LACROSSE

LACROSSE

THE PLAYER'S HANDBOOK

M. B. ROBERTS
PHOTOGRAPHS BY RONALD C. MODRA

STERLING

New York / London
www.sterlingpublishing.com

STERLING and the distinctive Sterling logo are registered trademarks of Sterling Publishing Co., Inc.

Library of Congress Cataloging-in-Publication Data

Roberts, M. B. (Mary Beth)
   Lacrosse : the player's handbook / M.B. Roberts ; photographs by Ronald C. Modra.
       p. cm.
   ISBN-13: 978-1-4027-4130-2
   ISBN-10: 1-4027-4130-8
   1. Lacrosse. I. Modra, Ronald C. II. Title.

GV989.R63 2007
796.34'7--dc22

                                            2007017055

10   9   8   7   6   5   4   3   2   1

Published by Sterling Publishing Co., Inc.
387 Park Avenue South, New York, NY 10016
Photos ©2007 by Ronald C. Modra
Text ©2007 by M. B. Roberts
Distributed in Canada by Sterling Publishing
c/o Canadian Manda Group, 165 Dufferin Street
Toronto, Ontario, Canada M6K 3H6
Distributed in the United Kingdom by GMC Distribution Services
Castle Place, 166 High Street, Lewes, East Sussex, England BN7 1XU
Distributed in Australia by Capricorn Link (Australia) Pty. Ltd.
P.O. Box 704, Windsor, NSW 2756, Australia

Book design and layout by Amy Henderson
Photography by Ronald C. Modra

Printed in China
All rights reserved

Sterling ISBN-13: 978-1-4027-4130-2
            ISBN-10: 1-4027-4130-8

For information about custom editions, special sales, and premium and corporate purchases, please contact Sterling Special Sales Department at 800-805-5489 or specialsales@sterlingpub.com.

CONTENTS

Author's Note

This book is primarily intended for young players—boys and girls under age 15 and high school athletes—their parents, and potential coaches and refs, so most of the discussion of rules, drills, equipment, and the like focuses on this level of play. We include college, club, and pro rules and information where appropriate, but our primary goal is to give young, aspiring players concrete direction and plenty of inspiration.

Although lacrosse players owe a great debt to Canada, for clarity's sake, this book is primarily aimed at players in the United States. Further, since field lacrosse is the version of the sport most often played in the United States, that is the emphasis here.

Throughout the book, US Lacrosse rules are quoted with permission; rules referenced verbatim are italicized. Most of the terms in the Coming to Terms section come from US Lacrosse rules and publications. Also quoted frequently are National Federation of State High School Associations (NFHS) Boys' rules. These are reprinted with permission and italicized when quoted directly.

So you want to play lacrosse? Contact US Lacrosse for a rule book appropriate to your level of play. Get a stick, find a field and get ready to play the fastest game on two feet.

FOREWORD

Lacrosse is one of the fastest-growing sports in the country. Why?

It's a fast-paced sport that combines some of the best elements of other sports, such as basketball, soccer, and hockey. You'll see picks and cuts, transition play, and deft handling of the stick. It's a sport that rewards both skill and raw athletic ability. It's a sport that embraces its participants in a supportive community.

Lacrosse also embraces its past. With a history that spans centuries, it is the oldest sport in North America. Rooted in Native American religion, lacrosse was often played to resolve conflicts, heal the sick, and build strength and virility in men.

Although the rich history and nature of the sport factors into its growth in popularity, simply getting a stick into a child's hand for the first time is what really gets the ball rolling. Once playing, the young athlete is usually hooked. It's just that fun.

US Lacrosse, established in 1998 as the sport's governing body, has played a leading role in the recent growth of the sport by providing critical resources to fuel the forward momentum. Every year, the US Lacrosse New Start initiative helps more than two hundred programs get started by supplying information and resources. The US Lacrosse Youth Equipment Grant Program recently provided more than $400,000 worth of equipment to start-up programs.

Recruitment and education of coaches continues to be a focal point for US Lacrosse and its Coaches Education Program, the sport's first nationally standardized program that has helped train more than twelve hundred coaches (and officials in similar programs) since its launch in 2004.

Maintaining the culture of the sport in a wave of growth represents a significant challenge, but US Lacrosse has met that challenge by forming a national partnership with the Positive Coaching Alliance (PCA). US Lacrosse is also developing a best practices standard to be implemented by lacrosse leagues around the country.

US Lacrosse is committed to ensuring player safety. Its Sports Science and Safety Committee has undertaken several lacrosse-specific research projects and is using findings from such studies to help make the game safer.

The growth of the game is undeniable. Nearly fifty thousand fans pack NFL stadiums on Memorial Day weekend to watch the NCAA men's championships. Two professional lacrosse leagues now feature franchises from coast to coast. At the high school level, more states formally recognize the sport each year. At the youth level, more than two hundred thousand boys and girls crowd fields across America each weekend.

It's never too late to learn to coach, officiate, or even play lacrosse. To learn more about the sport and to see how it might enrich your life, please visit the US Lacrosse Web site at www.uslacrosse.org.

Brian Logue
Director of Communications
US Lacrosse

Acknowledgments

Special thanks to the following people and organizations for providing guidance, inspiration, and/or know-how: US Lacrosse, especially Brian Logue and Bobby Bardzik; the welcomers at the US Lacrosse Youth Festival in Orlando; the National Federation of State High School Associations (NFHS), for granting permission to quote rules and reprint diagrams; Tori Leech, for her help in organizing the photo shoot with the teams from Carroll County, Maryland; coaches Jeff Beeker and Meagan Voight and all the players from Check-Hers Elite and Central Maryland Lacrosse who participated; Mark Hall, for demonstrating officials' calls; Tiffani Cone, for demonstrating conditioning moves; Dom Starsia, Missy Foote, Trish Dabrowski, and Jim Thompson, for their interviews; and Johns Hopkins' Associate Athletic Trainer, Matthew Bussman, Strength and Conditioning Coach, Chris Endlich, and Brian Yeager at Pro Strength in Philadelphia, for their expertise.

Our gratitude, too, to the following sources for research and/or quotations: US Lacrosse publications, including the *Parents' Guide to the Sport of Lacrosse* and *Coaching Youth Lacrosse; Lacrosse for Dummies;* and *Positive Coaching.*

Thanks also to the Roberts family typing team: Manda, Jordan, and Will. Thanks to Lauren for the inspirational drawings and to Howard Roberts for his always sage advice. And finally, thanks lacrosse players!

M.B. Roberts
Ron Modra

1: THE SCOOP ON LACROSSE

The Ins and Outs of America's Fastest-Growing Sport

So, you want to play lacrosse?

First, you'll need a stick and a ball, and unless you already have teammates, you'll also need a wall. Girls will need goggles, and guys will need helmets and other pads. You'll need a coach and a field. In some places you can play indoors, although the rules will be a little different.

Every player should have the desire to learn the rules and the moves of this fast-moving, high-scoring game. You'll need to run fast and run a lot.

Still want to play lacrosse? Get ready for a wild ride.

MUCH MORE THAN JUST A STICK AND A BALL

Lacrosse ("lax" for short) is the lightning quick, exciting game where ten players (twelve in the women's game) carry long-handled sticks with triangular pockets at the end to transport a ball downfield in an attempt to put it into their opponents' net. Offensive players run and pass to move the ball downfield and then shoot in an attempt to score. Then they switch into defensive mode to try to keep their opponents from scoring against them.

As the oldest continuously played game in North America, both Canada and the United States claim lacrosse as their original national pastimes. Native Americans invented the game and French missionaries, who saw settlers playing, gave it the name we use today.

In the 1800s, the game was embraced by non–Native American men in Canada and eventually spread to the United States. Today, lacrosse is played on five continents and is one of the fastest-growing sports in the world.

GROWING BY LEAPS AND BOUNDS

According to the national governing body of the sport, US Lacrosse, since 1995, the number of

Lacrosse players stick together.

More and more boys and girls are picking up lacrosse.

GROWTH SPURT

In Washington state, the number of boys' and girls' youth teams grew from fourteen in 2000 to eighty-nine for the 2005 spring season. Boys in the first grade are the youngest lacrosse players in the state.

Baltimore has long been known for its connection to lacrosse, but the sport is taking off everywhere in Maryland. Along the state's Eastern Shore, there were 2,285 players participating on 110 teams in 2005. The Western Maryland Chapter, one of the newest US Lacrosse chapters, had more than three thousand youth participants in 2005.

In Missouri, the number of youth players grew from three hundred players in 2001 to nearly two thousand in 2005. There are now seven leagues around the state, and play is available year-round.

In North Carolina, there were 410 youth players in 2001. Just four years later, the number of youth players across the state, from Wilmington to Asheville, increased to 2,375.

Courtesy of US Lacrosse.

X-FACTOR

Lacrosse is often described as an X-Games type of sport: exciting, fast, young, and very, very cool. Is it the outrageous uniforms? The eyeblack? The sticks? Or is it that in areas where the game is new, such as the South and West, many young athletes are playing a sport their parents don't yet understand?

As David Morrow, former U.S. national team player and founder of the lacrosse equipment company Warrior, told *Sports Illustrated*, "Parents aren't yelling as much on the sidelines because they don't know what's going on. Kids can really take ownership of the sport."

It's cool to be lax.

varsity high school programs has increased by nearly 200 percent; between 1994 and 2003, lacrosse expanded more than any other sport sanctioned by National Collegiate Athletic Association (NCAA). Although it has long been popular in the Northeast, especially in New York and Maryland, some form of lacrosse is now played in almost all fifty states.

WHO, WHAT, WHERE, WHEN?

Men, women, boys, and girls of all ages play lacrosse today. The rules vary depending on type of game, gender, and level of play.

There are three basic types of lacrosse.

1. Mini lacrosse (also known as "soft lacrosse"). Played by beginners, mostly young players in school gym classes. This is an extremely simple, modified version of the game where basic skills are emphasized. No body or stick checking is allowed.

2. Box, or indoor, lacrosse (also called "boxla"). This type of lacrosse originated in Canada in the 1930s to make use of ice hockey arenas (covered with cement or turf floors) during the summer. Athletes play six-on-six and use many of the same rules and equipment as hockey.

3. Field lacrosse. Both men's and women's versions of the game are played outdoors on football-sized fields, usually in the spring or the fall, although summer play, especially in camps, is becoming more common. Men play with 10 players on each side and wear pads and helmets because body and stick contact is allowed. The women's version is played twelve-on-twelve with no body checking and limited stick contact allowed.

No checking in the girls' game.

Youth, high school, and collegiate players in the Unites States mostly play field lacrosse, whereas box lacrosse is favored in Canada. Leagues are usually organized by age or level of play and by gender, because the men's and women's games vary a great deal.

Although lacrosse is mainly played in the spring, many colleges play Fall Ball, which usually consists of a lighter schedule, and some clubs also play in the summer. Box lacrosse is played year-round, depending on the league.

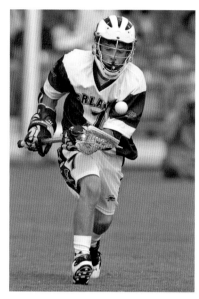

Lacrosse players take to the field.

YOU GO, GIRL!

Unlike soccer or basketball where the male and female versions of the sport are extremely similar, men's and women's lacrosse are two completely different animals. The reason for this is simple: men's lacrosse is a contact sport; women's is not. This means men wear a lot more protective equipment than women and follow an entirely different set of rules.

Lacrosse enthusiasts enjoy pointing out that the women's version of the sport more closely resembles the Native American game of the past; some modern women's teams continue to use wooden sticks and, until 2006, played without boundaries. Even with these recent changes, modern women and early Native American players still share several similarities: neither wear (or wore) pads, and both rely (or relied) on mass attack (over field positions) for their game strategy.

A women's team gets warm.

In women's competitions rules depend on age and affiliation. In college, women compete as part of the NCAA. In high school, scholastic teams follow US Lacrosse women's rules. Further, high schools will usually field both a varsity and a junior varsity team if there are enough interested players. If there aren't enough players for two squads, the school will just field a varsity team. This is true for both boys' and girls' games.

Boys and girls under the age of 15 play in youth leagues that follow US Lacrosse youth rules. The age divisions for girls in US Youth Lacrosse break down as follows:

ABCs

Figuring out who belongs to which lacrosse league, especially at the college level, can be much like staring into a bowl of alphabet soup. The US Lacrosse Intercollegiate Associates (USLIA), the association of college club teams that falls under the US Lacrosse umbrella, is often confused with the United States Intercollegiate Lacrosse Association (USILA), which is the association of schools with varsity lacrosse programs in all three NCAA divisions. (As of 2005, there were 213 members.)

In an attempt to avoid this confusion, US Lacrosse encouraged the USLIA to change its name to the US Lacrosse Men's Division Intercollegiate Associates (MDIA) to complement the US Lacrosse Women's Division Intercollegiate Associates (WDIA), but the men still mostly use the USLIA title.

Just to keep the soup simmering, as of 2007, the men's club teams began moving out from under the US Lacrosse umbrella to form a new group, the Men's Collegiate Lacrosse Association (MCLA). The women will stay with US Lacrosse.

Girls play by their own rules.

Youth leagues may decide on age level play that best suits their needs, within the following suggested guidelines: 6–8 year olds (Under 9), 9–10 year olds (Under 11), 11–12 year olds (Under 13), 13–14 year olds (Under 15).

The girls' youth rules are divided by levels (A, B, and C). Beginning teams/players would be expected to use Level B or C rules, which do not allow checking and do allow certain stick modifications to make throwing and catching easier. Players would then progress to Level A rules, which allow modified checking and require the use of a regulation crosse and pocket.

Any tournament play sponsored or sanctioned by US Lacrosse, such as the US Lacrosse Youth Festival, will use the following age and rule levels: Under 13—Level B rules; Under 15—Level A rules. Non-US Lacrosse sponsored tournaments should follow an age/rule level format and announce to participants prior to the tournament which level(s) (A, B, C) will be used at their event to avoid any confusion.

According to a 2005 *Sports Illustrated* article: "As parents discover that lacrosse is more exciting than soccer, cheaper than ice hockey, and not as dangerous as football, the game is getting a closer look."

BOYS TO MEN

Collegiate men playing for school-sanctioned teams compete in the NCAA. High school boys follow National Federation of State High School Associations (NFHS) rules. Players under the age of 15 follow US Lacrosse youth rules. The age divisions for boys in US Youth Lacrosse break down as follows:

Youth players will be age 15 years and under in grade 8 or below and further qualify as follows in order to participate in USL Youth Council

(USLYC) sanctioned youth lacrosse activities: (a) player has not attained 15 years of age as of December 31 in the year preceding a USLYC sanctioned event; and (b) the player has not participated in any high-school program as a member of a high-school freshmen, junior varsity, or varsity team.

Leagues may be organized by age or grades. Physical maturity should be considered when grouping players. If your program has enough players, the age/grade groups should play separately. The following is an example, with ages determined as of December 31 in the year preceding the USL Youth Council sanctioned event:

LACROSSE...
THE KEY TO SUCCESS?

Bold-faced names who once carried a stick:

Actors: **Tom Cruise**, **Michael J. Fox**, and **Judd Nelson**

TV reporters/personalities: **John Tesh**, **Geraldo Rivera**, and **Dick Schaap**

NHL players: **Wayne Gretsky**, **Joe Nieuwendyk**, **Gary Roberts**, **Colin Patterson**, and **Adam Oates**

NFL players: **Jim Brown**, **Patrick Kerney**, **Todd Sauerbrun**, and **Bill Curries**

Zach Thornton (Major League Soccer player)

Dr. James Naismith (inventor of basketball)

Bill Belichick (coach of the New England Patriots, three-time Superbowl champions)

Bruce Arena (U.S. Soccer coach)

George Tenet (former C.I.A. director)

Robert Mueller (FBI director)

Pete Coors (owner of Coors Brewing Co.)

John Kerry (Massachusetts senator)

Kurt Schmoke (former mayor of Baltimore)

Donald Schaefer (former mayor of Baltimore and governor of Maryland)

Orangeman Jim Brown.

Girls' lacrosse most resembles the Native American game of the past.

Senior Division: *Under 15/8th grade. May have competitive divisions grouped by ability.*

Junior Division: *Under 13/6th and 7th grade. May have competitive divisions grouped by ability.*

Lightning Division: *Under 11/4th and 5th grade. Non-competitive. Ages and grades may play together. Multiple teams within a program should be balanced.*

Bantam Division: *Under 9/2nd and 3rd grade. Non-competitive. Ages and grades may play together. Multiple teams within a program should be balanced.*

Many youth, high school, and collegiate teams for men and women are recreational (rec) teams or "clubs," meaning they are not funded by the school's athletic budget. In these instances, players must buy their own equipment and uniforms and pay for their own transportation. This also means they have a choice of which set of rules to follow. But for the most part, club teams follow the recognized guidelines for their age group and gender.

Nearly four hundred collegiate club lacrosse teams compete in an organized structure known as the US Lacrosse Intercollegiate Associates (USLIA). Many of these programs play on national schedules, and US Lacrosse conducts a national championship in three divisions for this level of play.

GLOBE TROTTING GAME

Internationally, lacrosse is now played in more than twenty countries on five continents: Asia, Australia, Europe, North America, and South America.

The International Lacrosse Federation (ILF), composed of nineteen member nations and nine affiliates, governs men's international play and organizes the World Championship, which is held every four years. (Upcoming event: 2010.) The ILF also conducts a U-19 (under 19) world championship every four years. (Upcoming event: 2008.)

Lax goes global.

OFFICIAL LACROSSE-PLAYING NATIONS

Argentina (ILF affiliate)	**Italy** (ILF)
Australia (IFWLA, ILF)	**Japan** (IFWLA, ILF)
Austria (ILF affiliate)	**Latvia** (ILF affiliate)
Bermuda (ILF affiliate)	**Netherlands** (ILF)
Canada (IFWLA, ILF)	**New Zealand** (IFWLA, ILF)
Czech Republic (IFWLA, ILF)	**Scotland** (IFWLA, ILF)
Denmark (ILF, IFWLA associate)	**Slovakia** (ILF affiliate)
England (IFWLA, ILF)	**Slovenia** (ILF affiliate)
Finland (ILF)	**South Korea** (ILF)
Germany (IFWLA, ILF)	**Spain** (ILF affiliate)
Hong Kong (ILF, IFWLA associate)	**Sweden** (ILF)
Ireland (ILF)	**Tonga** (ILF affiliate)
Iroquois Nation (ILF)	**United States** (IFWLA, ILF)
	Wales (IFWLA, ILF)

The International Federation of Women's Lacrosse Associations (IFWLA), consisting of ten member nations and two associate members, governs women's international play. The IFWLA organizes the World Cup tournament and a U-19 world championship every four years.

The ILF and IFWLA have plans to merge into one international governing body by the end of 2007. This bodes well for possible future recognition of lacrosse as an Olympic sport, as a unified international governing organization would be required.

Eight teams are scheduled to compete in the 2007 ILF World Indoor Lacrosse Championships in Halifax, Canada.

WHAT MAKES A GREAT PLAYER?

Are great lacrosse players born or made? The answer is both.

When we look at incredible players, especially those who are related—the famous Gait twins, Gary and Paul, for example—it may be

"PRO" LACROSSE FRANCHISES

As of 2007 there were some 575 pro lacrosse players in the United States and Canada.

Major League Lacrosse (MLL):

Baltimore Bayhawks
Boston Cannons
Long Island Lizards
New Jersey Pride
Philadelphia Barrage
Rochester Rattlers
Chicago Machine
Denver Outlaws
Los Angeles Riptide
San Francisco Dragons

National Lacrosse League (NLL):

Arizona Sting
Buffalo Bandits
Calgary Roughnecks
Chicago Shamrocks
Colorado Mammoth
Edmonton Rush
Minnesota Swarm
New York Titans
Philadelphia Wings
Portland LumberJax
Rochester Knighthawks
San Jose Stealth
Toronto Rock

Run fast and carry a big stick.

tempting to say that great lacrosse players are *born*. But then there is the current phenomenon in the sport: those talented athletes who played football or baseball as kids but then pick up a lacrosse stick late in high school, or even early in college, and excel. This makes a strong case for the "great lacrosse players are *made*" camp.

Lacrosse is a very intense, grueling endurance sport. So it seems that fast and agile athletes have the initial advantage. But players who are willing to put in the time for practice and conditioning can easily improve their game and compete with the best. In fact, because anyone can excel, lacrosse is a very democratic game. Unlike football, where size and bulk can give you an edge on the competition, or basketball, where a height advantage can make you a star, a lacrosse player need only be quick and good with a stick, both of which are skills that can be cultivated with training and practice.

There are also other democratic aspects of lacrosse. Everyone on the team gets many opportunities to handle the ball, and every player has a chance to score. And, although star players definitely emerge in lacrosse, the game is about how the team—not just one player—moves the ball down the field. With the exception of the goalie, lacrosse positions have many more similarities than differences.

> Most Division I All-America lacrosse players also played another sport in high school.

CROSSOVER SPORT

Enthusiasts often compare lacrosse to other sports or a combination of other sports. Centuries ago, English explorers saw Native Americans playing lacrosse, recognized a round ball, and compared it to tennis. Perhaps more accurate are comparisons between lacrosse and football, soccer, basketball, and hockey. Especially hockey.

Lacrosse and hockey use much of the same terminology, including *face-off*, *shoot*, *goal*, and the like. Also, in both cases, players carry sticks, pass frequently, and shoot at a goal to score. Obviously, lacrosse players toss a ball, not a puck, and they don't skate. But the speed, movement, and body contact of the players are quite similar.

It also makes sense that lacrosse and hockey go hand-in-hand, given both sports' close ties with Canada. The original rules of hockey, written in 1867, were patterned after those of lacrosse (written the same year), and many Canadian hockey players, such as Wayne Gretsky, also play or played lacrosse.

According to Syracuse coach Roy Simmons, Jr., the difference between football and lacrosse is that "Lacrosse is not eleven guys coming out of a huddle knowing what's about to happen. It's more fanciful, imaginative, and open."

Lacrosse is also often compared to basketball. Both sports have players moving down the field (or court) as a unit, passing as they go, and shooting at a goal (basket) to score. Many famous basketball players, even the inventor of the game, Dr. James Naismith, also played lacrosse. The good doctor even went so far as to call lacrosse, "The best of all possible field games." Enough said.

LACROSSE FRONT AND CENTER

Some athletes make lacrosse their primary athletic pursuit. The Lacrosse Hall of Fame, established in 1957 in Baltimore, is full of inductees who excelled in lacrosse first and foremost.

"CROSSE-OVER"

In terms of body contact and movement down the field, lacrosse has common traits with field hockey, ice hockey, football, basketball, and soccer.

Here's a little side-by-side sports comparison:

Like soccer . . .
lacrosse is played on an open field with goals at both ends.

Like soccer . . .
lacrosse features precision passes and often brings fans to their feet with the scoring of a goal!

Like hockey . . .
lacrosse players carry sticks and can move behind the goal.

Like basketball . . .
offensive lacrosse players set picks and run patterned offenses and fast breaks.

Like basketball . . .
defensive lacrosse players play man-to-man or zone.

Like football . . .
men's teams wear pads and do plenty of hitting.

Like ice hockey, football, basketball, and soccer . . .
men's lacrosse is a contact sport.

Looks familiar.

SIDE STICKS

Many athletes who succeeded in other sports also once played lacrosse. Wayne Gretzky, the National Hockey League (NHL) star known as the Great One, played lacrosse until he was 15. In a 2004 *Lacrosse Magazine* interview, Gretzky's father explains how lacrosse moves contributed to Gretzky's hockey strategy: "It sure helped Wayne, because in lacrosse, you learn how to fake, and he used those same fakes or moves in hockey."

Other NHL stars with lacrosse roots include Joe Nieuwendyk and Gary Roberts, teammates on the Calgary Flames and Florida Panthers, who were also lacrosse teammates (Whitby Warriors) during high school before they moved on to college and pro hockey fame.

Canada doesn't have a lock on famous athletes who played lacrosse. In the United States, the Cleveland Browns' running back Jim Brown was an All-America lacrosse (and football) player at Syracuse University before he went on to National Football League (NFL) stardom. Brown, who has been widely quoted as saying he preferred practicing lacrosse over football, was unstoppable with a stick.

"My size in lacrosse was uncommon and gave me a huge advantage," said Brown. "I weighed 225 my senior year (1957), playing midfield, where most guys were small. With my bulk and ability to match their speed, I could pretty much do what I wanted."

Composite Guide to Lacrosse

Before he took to the gridiron, Jim Brown carried a stick for Syracuse.

The Turnbull brothers, Doug Jr. and Jack, were early greats. Beginning in 1922, Doug was a four-time All-America at Johns Hopkins and later played for the prestigious Mt. Washington Club of Baltimore for thirteen years. Jack became known as the Babe Ruth of Lacrosse. He was a star attackman for the Mt. Washington Club and, as team captain for Hopkins, led his team to a second undefeated season in a row in 1932. That same year, Jack also played in an exhibition match at the Olympics.

Jack, who was killed in a crash while serving as a fighter pilot in World War II, is still remembered by the lacrosse community every year when the annual Jack Turnbull Attackman of the Year award is presented.

A few years later, another set of siblings made their mark on lacrosse. The Gait twins, from the Canadian Northwest, virtually revolutionized the game in the mid-1980s with their exciting, acrobatic style of play. "Up until Paul and Gary, we never had heroes in the game," said their coach, Roy Simmons of Syracuse. "They've been the Johnny Appleseeds of the game."

Gary Gait, who has been called the Michael Jordan of Lacrosse, was a four-time All-America at lacrosse powerhouse Syracuse. He went on to have an incredibly successful pro career in the Major Indoor Lacrosse League and then later in the National Lacrosse League (NLL). He was named league Most Valuable Player (MVP) three times, and in 2005, the Colorado Mammoth, the team he now coaches, retired his jersey, an NLL first.

Gary's brother Paul, born just 3 minutes after his identical twin, played alongside his brother all his life. He was a three-time All-America at Syracuse and scored the winning goal in a storied game against Penn, the same match-up where his brother debuted his famous "Air Gait" move—coming up from behind the net and dunking the ball over the top to score.

Early in the twentieth century, John R. Flannery, the father of lacrosse in the United States, expressed his admiration for the egalitarian nature of the game: "To lacrosse proponents, the distinctions between right fielder and third baseman or between defensive linemen and quarterback were far greater than those between first attack-man and cover point. With the exception of the goal tender, every player—and hence every gentleman—was an equal."

Great players are born and made.

The pro game is the top rung of the lax ladder.

Paul, who along with Gary was named co-MVP of the Mann Cup in 1999 when they played for the Victoria Shamrocks, also had a successful pro NLL career. He even came out of retirement in 2005 to play for the Colorado Mammoth alongside his brother.

THE PROS

Major League Lacrosse (MLL), launched in 2001, is a men's professional outdoor league consisting of ten teams that play a total of twelve games from May to August. The league has plans to add two more expansion teams in 2008.

The National Lacrosse League (NLL) is a men's professional indoor league, consisting of thirteen teams that play December through

February in both Canada and the United States. In 1998, the league merged with the Major Indoor Lacrosse League, founded in 1987.

There are many upsides to the fact that pro lacrosse is still a relatively new phenomenon. Players are almost always approachable before and after games and practices. They are also truly appreciative of their fans, giving autographs and running around the arena waving to their supporters after every game.

The pro game differs a great deal from youth, high school, college, and club lacrosse. The action is intense, and the rules are a little looser, so you'll see more fights at this level. On the positive side, there is also genuine respect between opponents, even after they've exchanged a few bruises during the game.

As the pro sport continues to grow, there will be a rise in regular TV coverage. In the meantime, fans may check scores and news about their favorite teams by visiting their Web sites or the Web site of the local newspaper from the team's hometown.

JOIN THE CROWD

A crowd of 19,432 watched the 2005 National Lacrosse League championship game between the Toronto Rock and Arizona Sting, setting a new league record. The game was also broadcast live in the United States and in Canada.

Syracuse University's Carrier Dome, an indoor stadium home to many of the best NCAA match-ups, seats fifty thousand fans.

A championship game record crowd of 44,920 watched the 2005 NCAA Men's Division I final between Johns Hopkins and Duke at Philadelphia's Lincoln Financial Field. The NCAA Division I men's basketball championship is the only other NCAA championship to have drawn more spectators. The largest ever lacrosse game crowd, 46,923 fans, gathered at Baltimore's M&T Bank Stadium to watch the 2004 NCAA Division I men's semifinals.

A crowd of 6,820—the largest ever to watch a women's lacrosse game in the United States—was on hand at Navy-Marine Corps Memorial Stadium in Annapolis, Maryland, for the championship game of the 2005 IFWLA World Cup between Australia and the United States.

Courtesy US Lacrosse.

2: BEYOND THE BALL AND STICK

The Story of Lacrosse

To truly appreciate the exciting modern sport of lacrosse, it may help to understand where, when, and how it all began.

Long before Columbus arrived on the shores of the New World, Native Americans were playing lacrosse. Although historians can't pinpoint the sport's exact date of origin—no records other than oral histories were kept during its earliest days—scholars agree that lacrosse dates back to the early 1400s, at the very least. Without question, it is the oldest continuously played sport in North America.

THE CREATOR'S GAME

Native Americans believed that the Creator gave them lacrosse for his own amusement. Thus, it was often referred to as "The Creator's Game." Players honored the Great Spirit at the start of every match, raising their sticks high before the face-off and yelling the spirit's name as they initiated play.

Native American players honored the Creator with their play. Courtesy of The Lacrosse Museum and Hall of Fame.

Games were frequently played during religious ceremonies and holidays and to mark the change of seasons. Tribes often staged matches to ask a god or force of nature to bless upcoming harvests or hunts. According to *The Composite Guide to Lacrosse* by Lois Nicholson, the Oklahoma Creek held a special lacrosse match as part of their Green Corn ceremony every year to mark the end of summer. The Ojibwa aligned lacrosse fields east to west as a tribute to the sun's sacred path, and the Cherokee, who revered water, always played their games near rivers and streams.

Some tribes played lacrosse to honor the gods. Others alleged that lacrosse was actually played by the gods. Nicholson writes that the

Cayuga believed in seven thunder gods who played lacrosse in the clouds using a bolt of lightening as their ball. Also looking skyward, the Abenaki thought the northern lights (aurora borealis) were actually their ancestors playing lacrosse in the heavens.

Some Native Americans took the additional step of enlisting assistance from higher powers, or their messengers, during games. Historians report instances of tribes hiring medicine men to perform rituals to help sway a contest's outcome.

A medicine man or shaman could earn his stipend by placing a turtle's hide in a dish behind a goal in order to bring the ball "home." Or, he might fashion a voodoo doll of sorts from beggar's lice, a plant with stems resembling human figures, name it after an opposing player, and pray over it to remove some of his strength.

As important as the spiritual element was to the early game, lacrosse was frequently played for more earthly reasons—a game of lacrosse could be used to settle a dispute over contested land. The game, nicknamed "Little Brother of War," was also regularly used to train young braves for battle. There is even a famous example of lacrosse being used to actually segue into battle, when in the summer of 1763, the Sauk and Ojibwa, led by Chief Pontiac, sought to capture Fort Michilimackinac (located in what is now Michigan) from the British, who had garrisoned the fort previously occupied by the French.

> Some Native American players elaborately painted their bodies prior to important matches, using red to signify combat, and wore feathers from birds of prey, believing they would adopt their keen eyesight and considerable strength.

Early Native American lacrosse games were often massive events with hundreds of players. Courtesy of The Lacrosse Museum and Hall of Fame.

During the English king's birthday celebration, when many of the soldiers were off duty, the two tribes organized a lacrosse game just outside the fort. Their women hid tomahawks, knives, and war clubs under their shawls and blankets and stood cheering near the main gate. As the game moved closer to the fort, a player threw the ball inside. At that point, the players dropped their sticks, grabbed the weapons from the women, and took over the fort.

Even when the game wasn't used as a prelude to battle, the early rough and tumble version of the sport was absolutely warlike. Besides the hard and fast rule that, with only a few exceptions, the ball should never be touched with the hands, there were virtually no rules.

According to Thomas Vennum, Jr., author of *American Indian Lacrosse: Little Brother of War*, maneuvers that would draw fouls today, such as tackling, wrestling, tripping, charging, ramming, slashing, and striking with the stick, were not only permitted but encouraged. Since they wore no protective gear of any kind, not even shoes, Native American players were almost guaranteed to emerge from a contest bloodied and battered.

Besides oftentimes being brutal, early Native American lacrosse was absolutely mammoth in scale. Teams consisted of up to one hundred or even one thousand players on a side. The goals, usually large rocks or trees, were anywhere from five hundred yards to a half mile (or even several miles) apart. There were no sidelines or boundaries, so players often spread out in every direction and played over hills and around other obstacles. Incredibly, these huge games lasted from sunrise to sunset and often spanned several days.

Historian Thomas Vennum, Jr., wrote that, "Playing lacrosse was preferable to armed conflict, and even in its early forms, was no more dangerous than football."

Although the Native American game displayed many similarities from tribe to tribe, Vennum highlights the nuances that existed in early lacrosse by breaking it down into three distinct regions: Southeastern, Great Lakes, and Iroquoian. Among Southeastern tribes, including Cherokee, Choctaw, Chickasaw, Creek, Seminole, and Yuchi, a double-stick version of the game featuring 30-inch (76-cm) sticks held in each hand and a soft, small deerskin ball cupped between them was (and still is) practiced.

Native Americans took pride in hand-crafting wooden sticks. Courtesy of The Lacrosse Museum and Hall of Fame.

Great Lakes players, including Ojibwa, Menominee, Potawatomi, Sauk, Fox, Miami, Winnebago, and Santee Dakota, used a single, 3-foot (0.9-m) stick that had a round, closed, 3- to 4-inch (8- to 10-cm) pocket that was just barely larger than the charred wooden ball.

Many Native American players were buried with their sticks so they could play lacrosse in the afterlife.

The Iroquois, as well as some New England tribes, played with the Northeastern stick or crosse, known to be the direct predecessor of all modern-day sticks used in both box and field lacrosse. According to Vennum, this stick [more than 3 feet (0.9 m) long] was the longest of the three types and incorporated a shaft ending in a sort of crook and a large, flat triangular surface of webbing extending as much as two-thirds of its entire length. The pocket was formed where the outermost string met the shaft.

THE EVOLUTION OF LACROSSE

The first white men to witness lacrosse were sixteenth and seventeenth century North American explorers and French Jesuit missionaries who came to the part of southeastern Canada known then as "New France" in the early 1600s. In 1636, one of the priests, Jean de Brebeuf, unknowingly launched modern lacrosse after watching a Huron tribe contest. He wrote letters describing a game where the natives played with sticks that looked like the "crosier" or "la crosse," the large cross that bishops carried in French churches. Hence the modern name of the game—lacrosse.

According to *Lacrosse, A History of the Game*, by Donald M. Fisher, Father de Brebeuf also wrote about instances where entire villages would play "a game of crosse" as a ritual to aid in healing sick people. Although North American Native Americans kept playing lacrosse and white men watched, it took a century or more for the game to catch on with transplanted European colonists.

By the early 1800s, white settlers in Montreal started enthusiastically playing lacrosse. During this time, strides were made toward making the sport more civilized, by way of introducing rules and a less violent code of conduct. Then, in 1867, W. George Beers, a Canadian dentist and avid lacrosse enthusiast, standardized the game by adopting a set of field dimensions, limiting the number of players per team, and formalizing other basic rules. Historians note that Beers formulated his widely

Modern lacrosse began in 1636 when a Jesuit missionary watched a Native American game and compared their sticks to a bishop's cross.

accepted standards after studying the ancient form of the sport and developing a philosophy that emphasized team play.

The Dominion of Canada was officially created on July 1, 1867, the same year Beers honed his rule book. Significantly, lacrosse was immediately named the new country's official sport, and Beers formed the Canadian National Lacrosse Association. Also in 1867, Beers organized a Native American team and a Canadian lacrosse club and made a trip to England, where they played an exhibition match for Queen Victoria at Windsor Castle—another historic lacrosse milestone. According to *The Composite Guide to Lacrosse*, the queen noted that the game was "very pretty to watch."

With the queen's nod and after further overseas trips for exhibition matches by Native American players from Canada, the popularity of lacrosse in Europe spread. Teams were soon formed in Scotland, Ireland, England, and France. And of course, in Canada's neighbor to the south.

When Canadian dentist W. George Beers standardized the game in 1867, one of his rules read that "no substitutions are allowed after a match begins, even if a player is injured."

LACROSSE IN THE U.S. OF A.

In the mid-late nineteenth century, lacrosse was also beginning to take off in the United States, primarily in the Northeast. Historians note that lacrosse gleaned its first mention in an American newspaper when it printed an article about an exhibition game by a Native American team at the Saratoga Springs fairgrounds on August 7, 1867—indeed, a very big year for lacrosse.

Later that year, a Native American team demonstrated lacrosse during a baseball tournament in Troy, New York. According to the author Lois Nicholson, the following day, the Native Americans played against the baseball team, and *The Troy Daily Times* reported that "thousands gained admission, and several hundred saw the game from the hills to the east."

Soon after this milestone, the first American lacrosse club, the Mohawk Club of Troy, was formed. Then in 1877, intercollegiate lacrosse officially kicked off when New York University, whose team was the first in the United States, played Manhattan College. (NYU won since they led 2–0 when the game was called due to darkness.)

High schools soon followed suit when, in 1882, three institutions fielded teams: Phillips Andover Academy in Massachusetts, Phillips

Princeton players, 1884. Courtesy of The Lacrosse Museum and Hall of Fame.

Exeter Academy in New Hampshire, and the Lawrenceville School in New Jersey.

According to *Lacrosse: A History of the Game*, in 1878 there were six or seven club teams in the United States. By 1885, there were more than one hundred and fifty, including twelve in New York City and up to thirty in Boston. The game also spread to areas in the states where Canadians had relocated, including San Francisco, Saint Paul, Milwaukee, Saint Louis, Chicago, Detroit, Cleveland, and, appropriately, LaCrosse, Wisconsin.

One of these transplanted Canadians, Irish-Canadian immigrant John R. Flannery, who later became known as the father of lacrosse in the United States, was perhaps the most effective emissary of the game in its early stages. After learning to play as a member of the Montreal Shamrock Club at age 16, Flannery moved to Boston in 1875 and, along with fellow expatriate Samuel McDonald, formed a team for the Union A.C. He then organized an amateur championship against New York City's Ravenswood Club on July 4, which his team won.

Flannery subsequently moved to New York and helped organize some nine other clubs in the state, thus initiating the movement that led to the formation of the United States National Amateur Lacrosse Association (USNALA) in 1879.

Then, in 1881, the first-ever intercollegiate lacrosse tournament was played, with Harvard topping Princeton 3–0 in the final. Soon after, in 1883, the Intercollegiate Lacrosse Association was formed, consisting of several prestigious universities, including Harvard, Yale, Princeton, New York, Lehigh, and Stevens Institute. It's interesting to

John R. Flannery, the father of U.S. lacrosse. Courtesy of The Lacrosse Museum and Hall of Fame.

note that although lacrosse was becoming popular at American colleges during this time, it was almost exclusively a club sport in Canada, which counted some forty-five clubs as part of the National Lacrosse Association as of 1887.

Despite the emphasis on college play, some new clubs and leagues were formed in the United States before the turn of the century. According to the author

Donald Fisher, in 1894, Brooklyn's Crescent Athletic Club was founded and became a dominant force in the development of lacrosse. The sport continued to grow as clubs and colleges in the New York City area formed the Metropolitan Lacrosse Association in 1885, and clubs based in Baltimore, Philadelphia, and Brooklyn formed the Eastern Association in April 1889.

In 1905, the Intercollegiate Lacrosse Association was succeeded by the Intercollegiate Lacrosse League (ILL), which changed its name to the U.S. Intercollegiate Lacrosse Association (USILA) in 1929.

Even the most avid lacrosse player or fan can't claim that lacrosse was the dominant sport at the majority of American universities in

Lacrosse put down deep roots in the Northeast.
Courtesy of The Lacrosse Museum and Hall of Fame.

Bristow Adams.

Johns Hopkins University was and is synonymous with lacrosse.
Courtesy of The Lacrosse Museum and Hall of Fame.

the early twentieth century. Still, there are some schools where lacrosse was, and is, king. Then and now, Johns Hopkins University in Baltimore is practically synonymous with lacrosse. In the 1890s, hockey was popular at Hopkins. Then, according to the Web site Hickocksports.com, some students, who learned lacrosse while visiting Long Island, introduced the sport to their prestigious Maryland school. Student athletes embraced the new game vigorously. Lacrosse fever soon spread through the entire Baltimore area, infecting players of all ages, and the city has been a hotbed for lacrosse ever since.

As explained in exhibits at the Lacrosse Hall of Fame, college teams such as Hopkins definitely transformed the game over the next few years. For instance, Hopkins center Ronald Abercrombie pioneered the use of a tennis net stretched between the goalposts to serve as a

In 1881, the first-ever intercollegiate lacrosse tournament was played, with Harvard topping Princeton 3–0 in the final.

backdrop. Later, he and his teammate William H. Maddren began using a shorter stick. When his teammates followed suit, the sport saw a dramatic rise in its short passing game.

GOING GLOBAL

The British have been playing lacrosse ever since Queen Victoria cheered at an exhibition of the game on her home turf in 1867. And it's not just male subjects who've embraced the sport. In 1890, the first women's lacrosse game was played at St. Leonard's School in St. Andrew's, Scotland. Over the next decade or so, lacrosse was adopted for English women, primarily as a springtime alternative for girls who played field hockey in the fall. American girls would have to wait, though. Although there were a few attempts to introduce the game for female players in the United States, U.S. women's lacrosse wouldn't really take off for another twenty-five years.

After the Brits began playing lacrosse, the game spread to Scotland, Wales, Ireland, Australia, New Zealand, and South Africa, among other places. Even so, only three countries—the United States, England, and Canada—sent teams to the 1904 Olympic Games in St. Louis, the year lacrosse debuted as an Olympic sport. The same three countries were invited to compete again in the 1908 London games, although this time, the American team, represented by Johns Hopkins, did not ultimately make the trip. Canada won the gold both times.

In the early 1930s, lacrosse experienced a huge revival in Canada, its country of origin, when box lacrosse, or "boxla," was developed.

Partially due to global events such as World War I and to the fact that many countries simply did not have enough quality players or a national governing body to administer a team, lacrosse was not featured in the Olympics for the next twenty years. But, in the years of 1928 and 1932, it was again included as a "demonstration sport."

In the early 1930s, lacrosse experienced a huge revival in Canada, its country of origin, when box lacrosse, or "boxla," was developed in order to make use of empty ice hockey arenas during the summer. This indoor version of the game, played with six-man teams on cement- or turf-covered rinks, incorporated many of the same rules

Bryn Mawr School lacrosse team, 1928.
Courtesy of The Lacrosse Museum and Hall of Fame.

Syracuse lacrosse team, 1923.
Courtesy of The Lacrosse Museum and Hall of Fame.

and equipment used in hockey. Although outdoor or field lacrosse was popular at the time, box lacrosse drew bigger crowds, a phenomenon that continues today.

SLOW AND STEADY

Back in the United States, the popularity of lacrosse continued its ebb and flow. The women's game got a boost when Rosabelle Sinclair started the first girls' team at Baltimore's Bryn Mawr school in 1926. Women's clubs in Baltimore, New York, and Philadelphia were subsequently formed and, in 1931, the United States Women's Lacrosse Association was founded.

On the men's side, the game experienced a series of ups and downs. For example, at the 1932 Los Angeles Olympics, lacrosse was again included only as an exhibition sport between just two teams, the

United States and Canada. On the positive side, more than eighty thousand people gathered in the stadium waiting for the conclusion of the marathon saw the U.S. Lacrosse Team defeat Canada.

"Lacrosse is the king of all field games."
—JOHN R. FLANNERY, THE FATHER OF U.S. LACROSSE

Over the next few decades, the most significant historical lacrosse milestones involved refining of rules and improvements in equipment. In 1933, in order to speed up the game, the number of players on a men's team was reduced from twelve to ten. The distance between goals was reduced from 110 yards to 80 (91.4 m to 73.2), and the playing area behind each goal was fixed at 20 yards (18.3 m). In 1947, the position names—formerly goalkeeper, point, cover point, first defense, second defense, center, second attack, first attack, out home, and in home—were changed to include just four: goalkeeper, midfield, attack, and defense. In 1948, the crease dimension was changed from a 10-by-12 foot (3.1-by-3.7 m) rectangle to a circle with a 9-foot (2.7-m) radius. In 1953, a rule allowing free movement after stoppage of a play was adopted; previously, players had been required to freeze at the sound of a whistle.

Other rule changes followed over the years. For example, in 1979 the face-off was eliminated from the men's game in

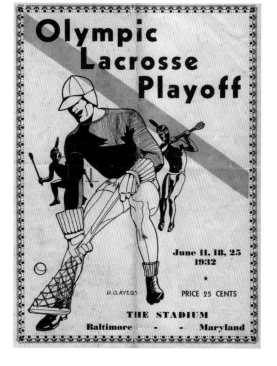

Program from the Olympic Lacrosse Playoff, Baltimore, Maryland, June 1932. Courtesy of The Lacrosse Museum and Hall of Fame.

an attempt to prevent cheating—it was reinstated the following year. Recently, restraining lines and boundaries were added to the women's game, resulting in a major shift in the way the game is played. The evolution of the rules has impacted the sport enormously, but without a doubt, equipment changes have had the most far-reaching effects.

In the early years of lacrosse, wooden sticks were handmade by Native American craftsmen. Players mostly bought sticks, often limited in supply, on or near reservations. This was one of several factors that kept lacrosse from exploding into the mainstream as baseball did.

In the early 1970s, the lightweight plastic head was introduced, and it immediately revolutionized lacrosse. By 1972, almost every player in the NCAA was using a wooden or titanium stick with a plastic head. Today, many styles of lightweight, inexpensive sticks are available in almost any sporting goods store anywhere in North America.

The titanium stick–plastic head combo revolutionized lacrosse.

FAST AND NOW

According to the US Lacrosse annual participation survey, there were about 400,000 lacrosse players in the United States in 2005. This figure was an enormous increase from the 250,000-plus U.S. lacrosse players listed in the 2001 survey. Further, lacrosse was the fastest-growing sport at both the high school and college levels nationwide according to data gathered by the National Federation of State High School Associations (NFHS) and the National Collegiate Athletic Association (NCAA). Perhaps most encouraging to the future of the sport, US Lacrosse also reported a sharp rise in its youth membership. The number of young U.S. lacrosse players grew from 40,000 in 1999 to over 100,000 in 2005. In contrast to 2005 US Lacrosse survey data, chapter survey estimates indicate there are actually some 200,000 youth players in the United States—quite an impressive increase.

Not surprisingly, much of the sport's growth is directly related to the surge in the women's game. This popularity was a direct result of the Title IX legislation, which provides parity for girls in sports, passed in the 1970s. Although more boys than girls play lacrosse nationwide, it's interesting to note that while fifteen states recognized high school boys programs in 2005, seventeen did so for girls' high school programs. Also, the growth of women's lacrosse at the college level over the last ten years was more than 83 percent, while men's programs grew at about 25 percent.

PROS

With its long-established base in North American colleges and community clubs, lacrosse has a deep tradition as an amateur sport. Throughout the last two centuries, most players regarded lacrosse as a pastime, not a profession.

But there have been several attempts over the years to ignite the pro game, beginning with the introduction of the Canadian Professional Indoor Lacrosse League in 1931. This was the brainchild

Lacrosse is played worldwide.

The explosion of youth, high school, and college players bodes well for the future of the sport.

of a hockey promoters who wanted to fill empty hockey arenas in the summer while also keeping their hockey players, who made up the lacrosse teams, in shape during off-season. The league only lasted one year, but indoor, or box, lacrosse ("boxla") was born.

Later, in 1968, the short-lived National Lacrosse Association began play with eight teams from the United States and Canada. The league folded in 1969. Then in 1987, the Eagle Pro Box Lacrosse League sprang into action with four teams. In 1989, it added two teams and became the Major Indoor Lacrosse League (MILL). In 1997, the National Lacrosse League, which had previously operated for one year in 1974 with nine teams in the United States and Canada, re-upped and merged with the MILL—forming the new National Lacrosse League (NLL). Today's NLL is a men's professional indoor league consisting of thirteen teams from the United States and Canada, including two 2007 expansion teams: New York Titans and Chicago Shamrocks. In 2006, the NLL marked a major milestone when the inaugural class of the NLL Hall of Fame was officially inducted in Toronto.

Back in 2001, fans of field lacrosse got a pro version of their sport when MLL began play. Today, the MLL has grown to include ten teams, including four 2006 season expansion teams: Chicago Machine, Denver Outlaws, Los Angeles Riptide, and San Francisco Dragons.

WORLD DOMINATION

Internationally, lacrosse is now played in more than twenty countries on five continents: Asia, Australia, Europe, North America, and South America. Even though the fastest game on two feet is staking its claim in many parts of the world, still, it has not been included as an official Olympic sport since 1908. Over the years, however, lacrosse has been featured as an exhibition sport in several Olympics, including the 1980 Los Angeles games. With the sport's enormous recent growth spurt, it's only a matter of time before lacrosse players return to the medal stand.

Many Native Americans are still playing the game. Although the Great Lakes version of lacrosse had mostly died out by the 1950s, the Iroquois and Southeastern tribes continue to play their own forms of the sport. In fact, in 1988, the six-nation Iroquois Confederacy joined the ILF as an independent country and continues to field very competitive teams. At the 2006 World Championship, the Iroquois Nationals placed fourth, just after the U.S., Canadian, and Australian teams.

Whether choosing aluminum or wood, every time a young player picks up a stick and tosses the ball across the field to a teammate, he or she is keeping a long tradition alive.

MILESTONES IN LACROSSE HISTORY

1636

Jean de Brebeuf, a Jesuit missionary, first documents lacrosse after seeing the Hurons play the game as a medicinal rite near Thunder Bay, Ontario.

1662

French trader Nicholas Perrot describes a Native American contest as "a certain game of 'crosse' which is very similar to our tennis. They match tribe against tribe, and if their numbers aren't equal, they withdraw some of the men from the stronger side."

1763

The Ojibwas and Sauks play a lacrosse game to divert the attention of British soldiers at Fort Michilimackinac (in present-day Michigan). The tribe then invades and takes over the fort as part of what would come to be known as Pontiac's Rebellion.

Even during matches that continued for days, Native American players seldom let the ball touch the ground.

Warriors often trained for battle by playing lacrosse.
Courtesy of The Lacrosse Museum and Hall of Fame.

1794

Samuel Woodruff of Windsor, Canada, witnesses the rematch between the Senecas and the Mohawks and notes: "Shortly before the game, the two sides arranged themselves in parallel lines facing each other, each on its own side of the field . . . a ball was placed in the center between the lines. A man from each team advanced to it and with untied bats raised it from the ground." By this time, teams consist of sixty players, and the goal size and field lengths have changed considerably.

1834

Indians from the village of Caughnawaga demonstrate their sport for some Montreal gentlemen. The event is reported in the newspapers, and for the first time, "white men" are interested in playing the game.

1844

The first documented lacrosse game between whites and Native Americans is played.

1867

Dr. William George Beers, the father of modern lacrosse, finalizes a uniform code of playing rules for the Montreal Club. Two years later, in 1869, he publishes the first book about the sport of lacrosse, entitled *Lacrosse: The National Game of Canada*.

The number of Canadian teams increases from six to eighty. Upper Canada College in Toronto fields the first college team.

1868

Fireball lacrosse, a nighttime version of the game played using a ball doused in turpentine and ignited, is briefly attempted. For obvious reasons, namely that the flaming ball quickly burned to a crisp, this brand of lacrosse promptly fizzles.

1874

The Montreal Club introduces men's lacrosse in Victoria, Australia.

1876

Queen Victoria watches and endorses a lacrosse game in Windsor, England.

1877

New York University fields the first college lacrosse team in the United States.

1879

John R. Flannery, the father of American lacrosse, establishes the United States National Amateur Lacrosse Association, comprised of eleven club teams from New York, Massachusetts, and Pennsylvania, including Harvard University and New York University.

1881

Harvard defeats Princeton in the first intercollegiate tournament at Westchester Polo Grounds.

The Lawrenceville School team, 1890. Courtesy of The Lacrosse Museum and Hall of Fame.

1882

Lacrosse is established in three prep schools: Phillips Andover Academy in Massachusetts, Phillips Exeter Academy in New Hampshire, and the Lawrenceville School in New Jersey.

1884

Stevens Tech in New Jersey begins the longest continuous fielding of a team in the United States.

In July, ticket proceeds from a game played on Staten Island between the first-ever All-America lacrosse team and the Toronto Lacrosse Club team are used to help pay for the base of the new Statue of Liberty.

1890

The first women's lacrosse game is played at St. Leonard's School in St. Andrew's, Scotland.

1894

The Crescent Athletic Club forms to "play for the pure enjoyment" and "raise the standards of the game." The Crescents become a catalyst in the revitalization of lacrosse in the United States.

1904

Lacrosse is first played as an exhibition sport at the Olympics in St. Louis. Canada defeats the St. Louis AAA team, representing the United States, for the championship.

1905

The United States Intercollegiate Lacrosse League is formed. Laurie D. Cox, William C. Schmeisser, and Charles Latting form a committee to develop a uniform code of operation for college lacrosse and divide the schools into North and South divisions.

1908

Lacrosse is played as an exhibition sport in the London Olympics. England loses to Canada in the championship game. Johns Hopkins University was to represent the United States, but does not make the trip.

1917

The U.S. Naval Academy begins a seven-year undefeated streak. In 1920 they allow only six goals in nine games.

1921

The offsides rule is instituted, requiring each team to keep at least three men in each half of the field, not including the goalkeeper.

1922

Dr. Laurie D. Cox introduces the annual selection process for a college All-America lacrosse team, an honor that continues today.

1924

University of Maryland defeats Navy, 5–3, in the midshipmen's first loss in forty-six consecutive games over eight years.

1925

Doug Turnbull, a Johns Hopkins attackman, becomes the first player to be named first-team All-America four times.

1926

Rosabelle Sinclair reestablishes women's lacrosse in the United States when she starts a team at the Bryn Mawr School in Baltimore.

1927

The "new" draw, in the air, is first tried in women's lacrosse and is still used today.

1928

Johns Hopkins University, representing the United States in exhibition games at the Amsterdam Olympics, is declared champion in round robin play against Canada and England.

1931

Canadian box lacrosse is developed to fill empty ice hockey arenas during the summer.

The US Women's Lacrosse Association (USWLA) is formed.

1932

Lacrosse is played as an exhibition sport at the Los Angeles Olympics. More that eighty thousand people at the Los Angeles Coliseum, who are waiting for the marathon to finish, also watch Johns Hopkins, the U.S. team, defeat Canada.

1933

The number of players on a men's team is reduced from twelve to ten.

The USWLA holds its first national tournament in Greenwich, Connecticut. Baltimore defeats Philadelphia, 5–1, in the championship game.

The First U.S. National Team is chosen by the USWLA.

Lacrosse has always been a high-scoring game. Courtesy of The Lacrosse Museum and Hall of Fame.

Women players celebrate a win. Courtesy of The Lacrosse Museum and Hall of Fame.

1935

The first United States Women's National Touring Team travels to England but never wins a game during the trip.

1936

The Victorian Women's Lacrosse Association is formed in Melbourne, Victoria, in Australia.

The first Wingate Memorial Trophy—named in honor of W. Wilson Wingate, a Baltimore sportswriter who played and covered the game—is presented to the USILA champion. Wingate is credited with calling lacrosse "the fastest game on two feet."

1940

The first annual North vs. South Men's Collegiate All-Star Game takes place at Baltimore Stadium. The North defeats the South, 6–5.

Men's field boundaries are changed to present day standards: 80 yards (73.2 m) between the goals with 15 yards (13.7 m) of clear space behind each goal.

1947

Position names in men's lacrosse are changed from goalkeeper, point, cover point, first defense, second defense, center, second attack, first attack, out home, and in home to goalkeeper, midfield, attack, and defense.

1948

Hand signals for men's officials are introduced. Also, the crease dimension changes from a 10-by-12-foot (3.1-by-3.7-m) rectangle to a circle with a 9-foot (2.7-m) radius.

1949

The English Women's Touring Team comes to the United States for a lacrosse coaching and teaching tour.

In 1964, *The Blue Book of College Athletics* called lacrosse "the fastest growing sport in the United States."

1951

Mt. Washington Lacrosse Club, the oldest established club team, loses for the first time in fourteen years to Maryland Lacrosse Club, 5–4.

U.S. Women's Touring Team travels to England on the RMS *Queen Mary*.

1953

A rule allowing free movement after stoppage of play is adopted; rules established in 1867 required players to "freeze" at the sound of the whistle.

1957

The National Lacrosse Hall of Fame inducts its first class.

Baltimore's St. Paul's School defeats Long Island's Sewanaka High School in a boys' game, 9–2, breaking Sewanaka's ninety-one-game winning streak.

The U.S. Women's Touring Team ties England.

The U.S. and English Women's Touring Teams travel to Australia.

1958

The F. Morris Touchstone Trophy is established to honor the Division I Coach of the Year. Touchstone coached for thirty-three years, twenty-nine of which were spent at the United States Military Academy.

1959

The Lacrosse Foundation is incorporated as the sport's national development center and archives. The key leaders are Claxton "Okey" O'Connor, William "Dinty" Moore, Caleb Kelly, and Gaylord "Peck" Auer.

The California Lacrosse Association becomes the first lacrosse organization on the West Coast.

1964

The Blue Book of College Athletics calls lacrosse "the fastest-growing team sport in the United States." Between 1952 and 1964, the number of men's college teams increases from forty-six to eighty-four.

1966

The Lacrosse Foundation establishes its first national office in the Newton H. White Athletic Center at Johns Hopkins University in Baltimore, Maryland.

1967

Coach Willis Bilderback of Navy wins his eighth intercollegiate title.

In celebration of the 100th anniversary of lacrosse, Canada hosts the first international men's tournament, featuring national teams from Australia, Canada, England, and the United States.

The United States, represented by the Mt. Washington Lacrosse Club, wins the first world championship.

1971

Men's college lacrosse allies with the National Collegiate Athletic Association (NCAA), which holds its first collegiate championship. Cornell defeats the University of Maryland, 12–6.

1972

The International Federation of Women's Lacrosse Associations (IFWLA) is founded.

1973

Four club teams from Colorado gather in Aspen to start what is now called the "Vail Lacrosse Shootout," the most prestigious club tournament in the world.

The 1972 U.S. Team defeats the Great Britain Touring Team on American soil, for the first time since 1913, by a score of 6–4.

1974

As a result of the success of the 1967 international tournament in Ontario, Canada, the International Lacrosse Federation is founded and hosts its first official World Championship in Melbourne, Australia. Australian Laurie Turnbull presides as the organization's first president.

1975

The first "National Champions" are crowned at USWLA National Tournament: Division A—Philadelphia First Team, Division B—South Second Team, Division C—South Fourth Team, Division D—South Fifth Team. The winners are awarded the President's Cup.

1978

The Lacrosse Foundation publishes the first issue of *Lacrosse Magazine*.

Johns Hopkins ends Cornell's forty-two-game winning streak.

1980

Henry Ciccarone of Johns Hopkins University is the first Division I men's coach to win three consecutive NCAA titles.

Penn State's women's team wins its third consecutive National Collegiate Championship.

1982

The Western Collegiate Lacrosse League is formed.

Trenton State University hosts the University of Massachusetts in the first NCAA women's championship.

The first Women's World Cup is played in Nottinghamshire, England. The United States defeats Australia in overtime of the championship, 10–7.

1983

The Lacrosse Foundation establishes an annual lacrosse festival, The Lacrosse International, featuring men's and women's games at all levels of play. In 1987, the event is renamed the Hall of Fame Lacrosse Classic.

1985

The Rocky Mountain Lacrosse Foundation becomes the first of many regional chapters of the Lacrosse Foundation.

1986

The Japan Lacrosse Association is founded.

The first National Schoolgirls Champions are crowned at the USWLA National Tournament: 1st—Pennsylvania, 2nd—Delaware, 3rd—Baltimore East, 4th—Baltimore West and Virginia.

Australia wins the IFWLA World Cup.

1987

The Major Indoor Lacrosse League revives professional box lacrosse in Baltimore, New York, Philadelphia, and Washington.

1988

The first Men's International Lacrosse Federation Under-19 World Championship is held in Adelaide, Australia. The United States defeats Canada, 12–5, for the championship.

The Iroquois Confederacy joins the ILF.

1989

U.S. Women's team wins World Cup over England.

1990

U.S. Men's Lacrosse wins third consecutive ILF World Championship.

Coach Roy Simmons, Jr., of Syracuse University becomes the first coach to win four NCAA titles.

1991

The Lacrosse Foundation and Hall of Fame Museum opens at Johns Hopkins University in Baltimore, Maryland.

1992

The National Junior Lacrosse Association founded.

1995

The NCAA 25th Anniversary Team is honored at the NCAA Men's Lacrosse Championship Final in College Park, Maryland.

Discussions on forming a national governing body begin.

There are nearly half a million lax players worldwide.

Over 72,000 fans attend NCAA Division I & III Men's Lacrosse championships.

The first International Federation of Women's Lacrosse Association Under-19 tournament is held at Haverford College in Pennsylvania. Australia defeats the United States, 5–4, to win the Maggie Boyd Trophy.

1996

US Lacrosse is founded and incorporated as the national governing body for lacrosse.

Trenton State University sets a record, winning its sixth consecutive, ninth overall, NCAA Division III Women's Championship (although the 1992 championship was later vacated).

1997

The United States defeats Australia (3–2), winning the IFWLA World Cup title in Edogawa, Japan.

University of Maryland coach Cindy Timchal wins her fourth NCAA Division I Women's Championship in six years (1992, 1995, 1996, 1997) by defeating Loyola College, 8–7.

1998

On March 14, the new Lacrosse Museum and National Hall of Fame are rededicated, completing the expansion of the US Lacrosse headquarters.

The National Lacrosse League merges with the MILL and begins play with eight teams.

For the first time in history, the USWLA institutes a restraining line in women's collegiate lacrosse.

2000

The Tewaaraton Award Foundation, in conjunction with the University Club of Washington, D.C., formally establishes the Tewaaraton Trophy to annually honor the top female and male varsity collegiate lacrosse player in the United States.

2001

The University of Maryland finishes an undefeated season (23–0) by winning its seventh consecutive, ninth overall, NCAA Women's Lacrosse Championship.

2002

It is estimated that organized lacrosse is played by nearly 300,000 people in the United States and an additional 90,000 players worldwide. All told, the game is played in over twenty countries, on five continents.

2003

US Lacrosse hosts the first unified ILF and IFWLA Under-19 World Lacrosse Championships in Towson, Maryland. U.S. Men's and Women's teams are crowned champions.

37,944 spectators watch Virginia defeat Johns Hopkins in the NCAA Men's Lacrosse Championship game at M&T Bank Stadium in Baltimore, Maryland.

2004

Professional indoor lacrosse expands westward and ten teams—Anaheim, Arizona, Buffalo, Calgary, Colorado, Philadelphia, Rochester, San Jose, Toronto, and Vancouver—compete for the 2004 National Lacrosse League Champion's Cup.

2005

The IFWLA World Cup is played at the United States Naval Academy in Annapolis, Maryland.

NBC televises the NLL all-star and championship games live, marking the first time profes-sional lacrosse is broadcast live on network television.

2006

The International Lacrosse Federation World Championship is played in London, Ontario in Canada.

The inaugural class of the NLL Hall of Fame is inducted, with honorees including league founders Russ Cline and Chris Fritz, legendary players Paul and Gary Gait, and the late Les Bartley, the winningest coach in league history.

More than one million fans attend NLL games during the 2006 season, breaking previous NLL attendance records.

A significant rule change is introduced to the women's game, which now includes hard boundaries on the field.

As of 2006, Stevens Tech in Hoboken, New Jersey, had fielded a varsity men's team for 122 years—the most of any college.

3: THE RIGHT STUFF

Gear for Guys and Gals

You don't need very much equipment to play lacrosse. Girls should have good cleats, a uniform, goggles, a mouth guard, a stick, and a ball. Boys, and goalies on girls' teams, need all of the above, plus a helmet and pads. Although no piece of equipment can magically transform an athlete into a star, most lacrosse players are sticklers for just the right stick.

STICKING POINTS

A stick, or crosse, is the lacrosse player's best friend. Like a baseball slugger with his lucky bat or a rock star with his favorite guitar, a lacrosse player gets mighty attached to his stick of choice. The parents of a third grader who just joined youth lacrosse tell a story of their son sleeping with his stick every night. The members of a girls' team flying to an out-of-state tournament opt to carry their sticks on the plane rather than stow them in checked baggage. A college senior patches his cracked stick with duct tape rather than buy a new, unfamiliar model. Some players even go so far as to name their sticks or decorate them with team decals or painted designs. Although they may not realize it, when players customize their crosses in this way, they are carrying on a long tradition.

Lacrosse historians document many instances of early Native American players decorating their sticks with feathers and bright strips of cloth. According to *The Composite Guide to Lacrosse*, the Ojibwas' sticks displayed the same serrated grooves as their drums and war rattles. The Cherokee carved the diamond markings of a rattlesnake into their crosses so, as they believed, players could strike quickly. The holy men of many tribes often rubbed players' sticks with special ointments for blessings and good luck.

From the earliest days of the game, Native Americans played with many different types of sticks that varied in size and shape from tribe to tribe. The earliest crosses, which had no nets, looked more like long ladles than today's modern lacrosse sticks. Balls were held in place courtesy of strands of animal sinew strung through holes, or in some cases, pockets were completely enclosed by wood. Eventually, sticks evolved to include nets of twisted bark or leather.

According to Thomas Vennum, Jr., author of *American Indian Lacrosse*, many early players, who often held their sticks in one hand, initially sized them by measuring the distance from their fingertips to the ground. The tribes that played with paired sticks, including some Iroquois, Creek, Seminole, and Yuchi, made sure one stick—and more importantly its pocket—was smaller than the other so a player could clamp them tightly together to cup the ball in place.

Primitive nets were primarily designed to catch and then hold on to the ball. For this reason, most pioneering Native American players rarely passed, instead holding on to the ball and running with it for long stretches.

Although for the first few centuries of the sport, lacrosse sticks varied in size, shape, and design, until the early 1970s all sticks had something in common: they were handcrafted from hickory wood.

Early Native American crosses looked more like ladles than today's sticks.

For over five hundred years, lacrosse sticks were always wood, usually bent and strung with leather and gut to form a pocket.

Throughout the late 1800s, and well into the 1900s, the majority of sticks were made by the Mohawk tribe or by other Iroquois craftsmen living mostly in New York State and southeastern Canada. Since sticks took up to a year to make, they were in limited supply. Donald Fisher, author of the *History of Lacrosse*, suggests this is one reason for the slower growth of lacrosse as compared to baseball, where mass-produced equipment was readily available.

Although some modern technology, such as metal carving and the use of bending tools, was added to the process in the early twentieth century, handcrafted sticks—most with a curved-end handle and a large, flat net extending over half the shaft's length—were still the order of the day. In the 1950s, Chisholm Lacrosse, a company located on the St. Regis Reservation on Cornwall Island, Canada, sold more than 95 percent of all sticks. The company's products, although finished in a factory, were still primarily handmade by Native American craftsmen.

But change was imminent.

The introduction of a flat stick with a large triangular pocket in the 1880s resulted in more dodging and passing in the game.

In the 1960s, almost all sticks were still made of wood.

PLASTICIZATION

In the classic movie *The Graduate*, a man pulls Dustin Hoffman's character aside, puts an arm around his shoulders, and dramatically whispers one word: "plastics." This scene would be perfect to kick off a documentary about lacrosse.

In the late 1960s, several American and Canadian companies were experimenting with synthetic materials for use in the manufacture of lacrosse sticks. Former All-America lacrosse player Dick Tucker, who became president of William T. Burnett

The stick doesn't make the man. Or the woman.

Company in Baltimore, was a pioneer in this effort. Tucker applied the knowledge he had gleaned from working with durable urethane materials used in shoes, car bumpers, and tires to the production of lacrosse sticks. Soon, STX, Inc., was formed to produce a new line of Adiprene urethane rubber stick heads mounted on ash or hickory shafts.

At the same time, Brine, Inc., was also experimenting with manufactured materials, such as plastic, fiberglass, and aluminum, with the goal of creating a lighter, more standardized, and inexpensive lacrosse stick. By the early 1970s, researchers at Brine learned about Surlyn, a strong DuPont plastic, and used it to manufacture their first plastic stick. Shortly thereafter, they also developed a molding technique

Boys' and girls' sticks vary slightly, mostly in terms of size and weight.

that created the basic draft shape that is standard in the majority of today's crosses.

Top lacrosse players in the United States and Canada embraced the new technology right away. Although some players, notably many women's teams, continued to use wooden sticks in the 1970s and even into the early 1980s, almost all lacrosse players now play with synthetic sticks, usually made of a titanium shaft and a plastic head.

The impact of synthetic sticks on the game has been enormous. Wooden sticks—though beautiful and, in some cases, considered pieces of art—were sometimes heavy and difficult to control. Because they were crafted slowly in just a few locations, they were expensive and difficult to come by. Also, their lack of uniformity made it challenging for players to find just the right stick for their size and level of play, and the wooden models tended to break or get damaged relatively easily.

Synthetic sticks have improved the game and helped bring lacrosse to the masses. Today, players can choose from dozens of models made by several well-known manufacturers and find them in sporting goods stores all across North America and Europe.

When choosing a stick, consider the following factors: weight, length, head design, and stringing style. But as every good attackman will tell you, the stick doesn't make the player. It's what you do with it that counts. Perhaps University of Virginia men's head coach Dom Starsia said it best: "The style of stick you choose is not going to have a lot to say about the kind of player you become. You don't need the fanciest gear to learn the game properly."

THE UPSIDE OF SYNTHETIC STICKS

As players know, buying a certain stick won't necessarily make you a star. Still, synthetic sticks have many advantages over their wooden predecessors. Synthetic sticks are:

- Less expensive

- Easier to find

- Easier and less expensive to replace

- Easier to match to your size, height, and skill level

- Lighter and easier to handle

- Easier to catch with

- Better balanced

- More durable

- Available in a wide range of styles

- Less likely to injure other players

- Standardized—sticks are consistent in size and shape

- Usable by left- or right-handed players

WHICH STICK TO PICK?

Today, there are dozens of stick models available. How do you know if you should choose an aluminum or composite handle? Should you buy a stick with a straight double-wall head, a pinched sidewall head, a forward canted head, or an open sidewall head? The answer: personal preference.

It's a great idea to go to a lacrosse specialty store or sporting goods outlet and pick up and hold a variety of sticks before you buy. Ask around. What are other players using? Check the Internet, and talk to your coach.

No matter what stick you choose, it must comply with the rules of your league. Here are stick specifications for US Lacrosse girls' and youth leagues and NFHS boys' leagues:

The Crosse: The crosse (lacrosse stick) is made of wood, laminated wood, or synthetic material, with a shaped net pocket at the end.

Boys: The crosse must be an overall length of 40–42 inches [101.5–106.75 cm] for attackmen and midfielders, or 52–72 inches [132–183 cm] for defensemen. The head of the crosse must be 6½–10 inches [16.5–25.5 cm] wide, except a goalie's crosse, which may be 10–12 inches

Stick with it: Finding the right equipment is key.

Star player turned coach Gary Gait has said, "A kid will walk around with a stick the way he might walk around with his skateboard, and he'll be the cool kid at school."

[25.5–30.5 cm] wide. The pocket of a crosse shall be deemed illegal if the top surface of a lacrosse ball, when placed in the head of the crosse, is below the bottom edge of the sidewall.

Youth (boys): The length of the crosse may be 37–40 inches [94–101.5 cm] for offensive players in the Lightning and Bantam Divisions and defensive players in such divisions may use a stick with a length of 37–72 inches [94–183 cm].

Girls: The crosse must be an overall length of 35½–43¼ inches [90–110.5 cm]. The head of the crosse must be 7–9 [17.75–23 cm] inches wide. The pocket of the stick must be strung traditionally; no mesh is allowed. The top of the ball when dropped in the pocket must remain even with or above the sidewalls. The goalkeeper's crosse may be 35½–48 inches [90–122 cm] long. The head of the crosse may be mesh and up to 12 inches [30.5 cm] wide.

Youth (girls): Level C may use a youth stick with mesh or traditional stringing or regulation women's crosse and may have a modified pocket. With a modified pocket, only half the ball may fall below the bottom of the sidewall. Level B must use a regulation women's crosse with either a regular or modified pocket. Level A must use a regulation women's crosse with regular pocket.

Equipment rules, like playing rules, are very different for box lacrosse. For instance, box sticks are smaller, shorter, and narrower, and there are no restrictions on pocket depth.

STARTER STICKS

Not all sticks are created equal. A beginner should know what to look for when choosing a first crosse.

Stick type. Most players these days use aluminum- or titanium-handled sticks with plastic heads, although other combinations, such as wood, fiberglass, or plastic shafts and wood heads, are allowed.

Beginners often choose slightly thinner sticks made of aluminum—slightly less expensive and heavier than titanium—until they get the feel of the game and graduate to higher-end goods. Also, women's stick shafts are narrower than men's.

Stick length. High school and college rules for boys and girls set minimum stick lengths (see above), so beginners at these levels need to be mindful of the parameters. Youth players are allowed to use smaller sticks and should select one appropriate for their size. A beginning youth player should choose a stick with a shaft as long as her arm. As a player's game level advances, she can move to a larger stick.

Many players string their pockets themselves.

TIP: Defensemen normally carry sticks that are longer than those of offensive players. It's important that a player who wants to use a very long stick [72 inches is 6 feet (1.8 m)] can safely handle it. Remember, if you find yourself choking up too much on the grip, the stick is probably too long for you.

Pocket type. Although the rules for pockets at the high school level and above are more restrictive, beginning youth players have some flexibility. A soft mesh pocket is an excellent choice for a beginner since it makes catching and throwing easier. Traditional strung pockets tend to be more difficult to break in. As a player improves, he or she can switch to a traditional strung pocket or take the intermediate step of trying out a pocket with a medium-hard mesh.

Pocket size. The pockets on boys' sticks are allowed to be deeper than in the girls' game, but a too-deep pocket may cause problems. For example, the ball might catch on the strings and hook down toward the ground during a pass. Plus, an overly deep pocket (see above) may be ruled illegal. For best results, shoot for a pocket size that measures the diameter of one ball, or slightly less.

Former Cornell star and US Lacrosse Hall of Fame inductee Eamon McEneaney compared breaking in a wooden stick to courting a sweetheart.

TIP: To determine if your pocket abides by the rules, try holding your stick parallel to the ground at eye level with a ball in the pocket. If it is not below the bottom edge of the sidewall, you're in compliance.

Head type/size. Although there are many brands and head types to choose from, head sizes are similar for sticks used in field lacrosse. Plus, heads tend to have really cool names, such as the Gait Chaos Strung Lacrosse Head or the Brine Nitrous Unstrung. Offset heads, where the head is set back from the handle, are a top choice for all levels of players these days, since the pocket can be a bit deeper while still allowing the player to release the ball with a high velocity and trajectory. Pinched heads are also popular, but beginners should stick with a more open head at first. This will make it easier for players to learn to catch and release the ball.

TIP: Most lacrosse stick heads are flat when you buy them. Many players string the pockets themselves after purchasing a mesh pocket kit or leather stringing kit. New players may want to ask a lacrosse shop employee, more experienced player, or coach to do it for them the first time. Custom stringing is featured on many Web sites.

As you customize your crosse, remember that it is illegal to alter sticks in such a way that they give you an unfair advantage in the game. Keep in mind that the ref will inspect your stick before a game.

HOW MUCH?

Although an experienced player may prefer to customize his stick by buying the shaft and head separately—sometimes stringing his own pocket or weaving in his own shooting string—lacrosse retailers do sell complete sticks, where the pre-strung head and shaft come as a unit. Complete sticks are great for beginners who don't yet have a preference for certain materials or particular equipment. Retailers also offer starter packages that include a complete stick, ball, and protective

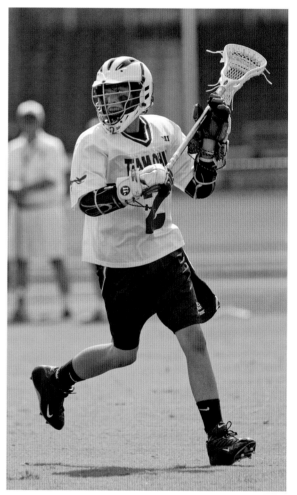

In lax, deep pockets can be a bad thing.

equipment. These packages are usually less expensive than buying equipment á la carte.

Starter packages cost approximately $75 for girls and $200 for boys. Other prices include:

Complete sticks: $35–$120

Shafts: $40–$180

Heads (strung or unstrung): $40–110

Goalkeepers' sticks, shafts, and heads usually cost a little more.

GOALIE'S STICKS

All-important goalies wield a stick with a much bigger head than a field player's—they need to use it to stop the other team from scoring. A goalie's goal is to try to save shots with the stick, using the body and protective equipment as Plan B. It is crucial for goalies to use crosses they

are comfortable with. Most goal-keepers choose plastic sticks, which are light and easy to handle, despite being long in length. Also, goal-keepers on both girls' and boys' teams have more latitude regarding pocket material, depth, and length of stick. Unlike field players, goalies aren't penalized for overly deep pockets.

TIP: A goalkeeper should aim to have his pocket in the upper-middle part of the stick to allow for a quick release of the ball.

Goalies carry the biggest sticks.

BALLS

Girls battle over a game ball.

Lacrosse prides itself on being a quick-moving game. It's actually written into the rules that the home team is responsible for placing a row of perfectly-spaced balls at the end lines behind the goal before the start of a game. That way, no time is wasted when the need arises for a fresh ball. Keep it moving!

According to US Lacrosse and NFHS rules:

(Men and boys, including youth): The ball must be made of solid rubber and can be white, yellow or orange. The ball is 7¾–8 inches [19.7–20.3 cm] in circumference and 5–5.25 ounces [141.75–149 g].

(Women and girls, including youth): May use a solid yellow regulation ball or a "soft" ball. It is highly recommended that new or beginner programs use the soft ball until players have developed their throwing and catching skills. If a soft ball is used, it should be approximately the same size as a regulation ball.

READ THE FINE PRINT

US Lacrosse rules further specify that regulation balls must have a bounce of not less than 43 inches (1.1 m) or more than 51 inches (1.3 m) when dropped from 72 inches (1.8 m) onto concrete at a temperature of approximately 65 degrees Farenheit (18 degrees Celsius) to 75 degrees Farenheit (23 degrees Celsius).

A regulation ball may be used for indoor play, however a "no bounce" ball is recommended.

Also, as of 2007:

The ball must be smooth—no dimpled balls may be used as game balls.

Although many players refer to modern lacrosse balls as *Indian rubber balls*, they have little in common with the early native variety. Ever since the Canadian William George Beers standardized the rules and equipment of lacrosse in the mid-1800s, the hard rubber ball, as opposed to the hair-stuffed deerskin ball, has been in favor. Certainly, a rubber ball can bruise a player, but picture early Native American athletes—who wore no pads—taking a hit from a solid wooden ball made from the knot of a tree or from a hard clay, hide-covered ball.

Modern lacrosse balls are inexpensive ($2.50–$3.00), and practice balls come in fun colors such as pink or red. Some even glow in the dark. Players may want to try weighted training balls to use during drills.

> A few years ago, a rumor had it that the NCAA was considering dyeing lacrosse fields lime green to spice up the game. Although this didn't happen, the NCAA did approve the use of lime-green balls.

NOTE: Girls play with yellow balls, but even though yellow or orange balls are legal, most boys' games are played using white balls. It is the home team's responsibility to assign a ball boy. However, ball boys may be waived if coaches from both sides agree.

THE EVOLUTION OF LACROSSE EQUIPMENT

Shorter sticks meant better play. Courtesy of The Lacrosse Museum and Hall of Fame.

1776

In his book *Travels*, English explorer Jonathan Carver writes that Native Americans played lacrosse with balls slightly bigger than tennis balls.

1794

Samuel Woodruff of Windsor, Canada, witnesses the rematch between the Senecas and the Mohawks and notes: "Shortly before the game, the two sides arranged themselves in parallel lines facing each other, each on its own side of the field . . . a ball was placed in the center between the lines. A man from each team advanced to it and with untied bats raised it from the ground." By this time, teams consist of 60 players and the goal size and field lengths have changed considerably.

1856

The Montreal Lacrosse Club is formed and becomes the first organized Canadian team to play under its own rules and with its own sticks.

1867

Dr. William George Beers, the father of modern lacrosse, finalizes a uniform code of playing rules for the Montreal Club. He also sets new standards for equipment by replacing the hair-stuffed deerskin ball with a hard rubber ball and introduces a stick that is better suited to catching the ball and throwing it accurately.

1898

William H. Maddren and Ronald T. Abercrombie of Johns Hopkins develop shorter sticks, which gives rise to the short passing game.

Centuries ago, the Creeks stuffed lacrosse balls with inchworms, which were invisible to birds, so the balls would also be invisible to their opponents.

1900

The cost of lacrosse equipment evolves. Youth sticks retail for $1.50, the "Flannery Celebrated Lacrosse Stick" or the "Lally Extra Special Stick" costs $4.00, and gloves go for $2.00.

1912

In England, the cost of a women's lacrosse stick is 6 shillings 6 pence.

1923

The cost of lacrosse equipment increases. Lacrosse sticks retail for $10.00, gloves for $9.00, lacrosse caps for $2.25, and lacrosse shoes or cleats for $3.50 a pair.

1937

Robert Pool introduces the first double-walled, wooden stick, an early prototype for today's plastic sticks.

1970

The NCAA Lacrosse Championship game was played almost entirely with wooden sticks. The next year, the same game was played using all synthetic sticks.

PROTECTIVE EQUIPMENT FOR GIRLS

In lacrosse, the major difference between boys' leagues and girls' leagues is that the boys play a contact version of the sport and the girls do not. For this reason, girls, with the exception of the goalkeeper, do not wear pads.

US Lacrosse publishes an extremely detailed list of dos and don'ts for what women and girls can and can't wear on the field—for example, because of safety concerns, girls are not allowed to wear jewelry.

Women's protective gear has greatly reduced injuries.

INJURIES

The US Lacrosse Sport Science and Safety Committee sponsors research that monitors injuries and studies their mechanisms in an effort to design preventive programs. Some of these studies have found both men's and women's lacrosse to be relatively safe compared to other commonly played team sports.

In game situations, there are fewer incidents of injuries in men's lacrosse than in football, wrestling, soccer, and hockey, according to NCAA Injury Surveillance System data. In women's lacrosse, there are fewer incidents of injuries in game situations than in basketball, field hockey, gymnastics, ice hockey, and soccer.

Although serious injuries can and do occur in lacrosse, most are relatively minor strains, sprains, and contusions.

In sum:

Protective equipment—mouthguards and eyewear are mandatory at all levels. Close fitting gloves are permitted, as is soft headgear; no hard helmets except the goalie. Goalie must wear helmet with face mask, separate throat protector, chest protector, goalie gloves, and leg padding on the shins and thighs. Protection for the abdominal area for goalies is strongly recommended. All protective devices used should be close fitting, padded where necessary, and not be of excessive weight.

EYEWEAR

Even though women's lacrosse is technically noncontact, unintended damage—courtesy of fast-moving rubber balls and errant sticks and elbows—can and does happen. For this reason, all female players always wear protective eyewear or goggles. On their Web site, US Lacrosse lists accepted brands and models, plus exact standards that they are required to meet. For instance, eyewear must withstand forces generated by a ball traveling 45 mph for youth play and 60 mph for adult play.

**Mouth guards
are mandatory.**

The good news is goggles look pretty cool and come in many different colors, often matched to a team's uniforms. A pair will cost you $30 to $60.

Mouth Guards

Like eyewear, mouth guards are a very important and mandatory piece of safety equipment for both girls and boys. Players are not permitted to even step onto a game field unless a mouth guard, which fully covers the upper jaw and teeth, is in place. As with eye goggles, mouth guards come in a variety of colors. In fact, NFHS rules state that mouth protectors should be a *highly visible color* and *may not be clear or white*. Guards can be purchased from a dentist or from a lacrosse or sporting goods store for $2 to $20.

Female players may also wear close-fitting gloves, close-fitting sweatbands, soft headgear, or noseguards if they like. If you opt to wear any of these items make sure they don't get in your way or endanger other players. Also, no female player, except for the goalie, is allowed to wear a helmet.

Optional but cool: Some players wear eyeblack, sometimes smearing it in the shape of intimidating triangles (as Syracuse star Michael Powell used to do) to reduce the glare under their eyes.

THE COST OF LACROSSE

Since guys have to wear helmets and pads, the cost of a complete lacrosse getup, including a uniform, shoes, stick, and all protective equipment, can run anywhere from $500 to $700—male goalies can spend up to $800; female goalies can expect to pay $300 to $450. If you're looking to save some cash, use equipment from other sports, such as hockey gloves or soccer shin guards.

Goalies need to cover it up.

PROTECTIVE EQUIPMENT FOR BOYS

Because men's and boys' lacrosse is a contact sport that allows full stick checking, male players are required to wear more protective equipment than female players. No player wants to feel restricted in his movements or hit the field looking like the Michelin Man. So, today's players shoot for a "less is more" approach whenever possible, gravitating toward technically advanced, less bulky gear. High school players must wear:

- Mouth guard
- Protective helmet
- Face mask
- Protective gloves
- Shoulder pads
- Arm pads

High school and youth players are also advised to wear a protective cup, rib pads, and kidney pads. Some players also wear elbow pads.

EQUIPMENT TIPS

- Choose gloves that fit well. Leather tends to last longer than nylon.
- Consider an all-in-one, three-piece pad to protect forearms, elbows, and biceps.
- Put your kidney pads on first so the other layers of equipment will help hold the shoulder straps in place.
- To keep your gear stink- and mildew-free, hang up and air out your equipment after every game. Hand wash protective equiptment with a mild detergent and then hang it up to dry.
- Treat yourself to a cool equipment bag, large enough to tote all your stuff.

The right coverage.

THE RIGHT FIT

US Lacrosse rules state that helmets designed for lacrosse and worn by athletes playing by its rules must meet the National Operating Committee on Standards for Athletic Equipment (NOCSAE) test standards. Players should also keep in mind that helmets must fit properly in order to do their very important job of keeping athletes safe. The Bicycle Helmet Safety Institute, provides the following fitting tips applicable for most sporting and recreation helmets:

1. The helmet should touch your head comfortably on all sides. It should fit snugly, so that it stays in place even when you shake your head violently. Some have pads that can move to fill gaps between your head and your helmet.

2. The helmet should sit level on your head, with the front just above the eyebrows. If you wear glasses, the helmet should sit just above the frames. The helmet's front rim should be barely visible when you look upward.

3. Tighten the chinstrap so that when you open your mouth wide, you feel the helmet pull down a little. The "Y" on the straps that run down the sides of your head should fit just below your ears.

4. Test the fit by pushing up and back on the front rim. If your helmet moves more than an inch, you need to tighten the Y-section of the chinstrap that runs in front of your ears. Push forward and up on the back rim. If your helmet moves more than one inch, tighten the Y-section in back of your ears.

GET IN UNIFORM

Besides those all-important pads, players also need game day uniforms. Guys wear shorts and jerseys, usually made out of poly-spandex or poly-knit waffle material, that are large enough to fit over their upper body pads but aren't so baggy that they get in the way. Girls pair jerseys with shorts, skirts, or a combination of the two called "skorts." Some girls' teams even wear all-in-one dresses, depending on the team's preference.

CUSTOM GEAR

US Lacrosse and NFHS rules have very specific guidelines for team uniforms that coaches and players should check before ordering custom gear. For instance, the boys' rules state that collars, cuffs, and waistbands may be of a contrasting color to that of the body of the jersey, but may be no more than two inches wide. But don't let the rules squelch your inspiration. Lacrosse jerseys are known for their vibrant colors and fierce designs.

Team members are also required to dress uniformly, although the goalie can wear a different top as long as it's the same color as the team's. Boys' team goalies need to make sure their jerseys are worn on the outside of their pads. Also, if male

Show your colors.

FEET FIRST

Choosing the right shoe may prevent painful ACL tears and other noncontact injuries. Matthew Bussman, Associate Athletic Trainer at Johns Hopkins University, recommends the following shoes for different playing surfaces:

Grass: Moldable or replaceable cleats

Astroturf: Tennis shoes or turf shoes

Sports turf: Turf shoe or molded cleat (for dry fields) and longer, molded replaceable cleats (for wet fields).

Shoe in: Be sure to choose the best footwear.

The best players use their heads on the field.

STX, the popular lacrosse equipment manufacturer's name, is a punchy abbreviation of the word "sticks."

players have shirts that are longer than the waistband, they are supposed to tuck them in.

One place to dare to be different: your feet. Players may wear any color shoes, and socks, they choose. They also have plenty of leeway as far as style. Running shoes or cleats (without spikes) for outdoor play and turf shoes for indoor play are acceptable. Because lacrosse players need ankle support, trainers highly recommend staying away from low-cut shoes. Also, seek out a perfect fit: a too-big or too-small shoe can cause blisters.

Players also have a chance to show their individuality during practice. Training clothes are shorts with jerseys, sweatshirts, or t-shirts. Many athletes these days buy workout apparel made with microfiber fabrics that wick the sweat away from the skin and dry quickly. Some uniform pieces are also made of this material, for instance, Ultralyte goalie pants.

Lastly, it is usually the home team's responsibility to makes sure the competing teams are wearing contrasting colors and should provide pinnes, if needed.

GOALIE GEAR

A goalie should always try to defend the goal with her stick, although sometimes, she has to use her body to make the save. That's why it's so important for goalies to be outfitted in properly fitted, regulation protective equipment.

Every team needs a goal.

US Lacrosse youth rules state that goalies must wear:

- Mouth guard
- Helmet with face mask
- Throat protector
- Chest protector
- Abdominal and pelvic protection
- Goalie gloves
- Leg padding on shins and thighs

Women's rules list the following required equipment:

- Mouth guard
- Helmet with face mask
- Throat protector
- Chest protector

The goalkeeper may also wear padding on her hands, arms, legs, shoulders, and chest as long as it does not excessively increase the size of those body parts. A goalie's pads should conform to her body as much as possible.

No whining! A goalie posts up.

TIPS FOR GOALIES

- Goalies' gear can be expensive, so if an athlete has equipment from another sport, she may also use it for lacrosse if it satisfies all the rule requirements. For example, a goalie may wear canvas field hockey leg pads or even her brother's football shoulder pads if they do not exceed the maximum legal thickness of 1 inch.

- A goalie can cover up as much as she wants, as long as she feels loose and agile in her protective gear. For example, a great addition to required gear is a wraparound throat protector, like the ones worn by field hockey players, to shield that vulnerable area. A well-protected goalie is a confident, effective goalie.

GOALS

Last, but by no means least, to play lacrosse, each team needs a goal—and we don't just mean the objective to win. Guidelines for the men's and women's games are similar: both state that game goals should consist of two wood or metal 6-foot (1.8-m) posts or pipes placed 6 feet (1.8 m) apart. The goal should be strung with netting in such a way as to prevent the rebounding of the ball. Also, goals need to be securely pegged down. Women's goalposts should be solid white, orange, or silver, while men's should be orange.

Youth rules vary slightly in that smaller cages may be used for indoor play and for Level C (girls) playing outdoors. It's important to check specific rulebooks for exact specifications of goals for your league.

US LACROSSE TIP: The use of three-sided goals sunk firmly into the ground with no backstays is recommended for grass fields. Goals with flat supports are recommended for turf fields.

Got net? Players who just can't get enough of lacrosse may want to invest in a practice goal or a shot trainer (a smaller net for practicing shots) to use on their own. A simple backyard goal costs under $150, and shot trainers can be had for $100. Another possibility: Consider buying a ball returner, a net that "shoots" the ball back to you, for $100.

PLAYING EQUIPMENT

Crosse: A lacrosse stick. Consists of a head, pocket, and shaft.

Goal: The netted backdrop that players shoot the ball into in order to score. Also, the term for successfully completing such a score.

Handle (shaft): An aluminum, wooden, or composite pole connected to the head of the crosse.

The hands have it.

Head: The plastic or wood part of the stick connected to the handle and strung with nylon or leather vertical thongs cross-woven with gut or nylon strings.

Long stick: Another term for defensive players' sticks that can measure up to 72 inches (183 cm) in length.

Pocket: The strung part of the head of the stick that holds the ball.

Shooting strings: Usually between one and four nylon strings (or shoe strings) that stretch across the widest part of the head to provide a smooth release of the ball from the pocket. Players often lace in these strings themselves.

Stick depth: How deep the pocket is.

Synthetic sticks: Crosses fashioned from manufactured materials such as aluminum or titanium.

Throat: The bottom, curved part of the head.

PROTECTIVE EQUIPMENT

Chest protector: A goalie's thick chest pad worn to protect the chest and help him stop shots.

Chin strap: A strap that fastens to the helmet and holds it in place. Required for youth players and recommended for all players.

Kidney pads: Crucial padding worn to protect the vulnerable kidney area, often exposed when a player's back is turned.

Mouth guard: The plastic mouthpiece, in a color other than clear or white, which every player is required to wear.

Pelvic protector: Pads worn by the goalie to protect the groin area.

Shin guards: Leg pads worn to protect the goalie's legs, sometimes used to stop shots.

Throat protector: Crucial piece of equipment that hangs down from the bottom of the cage (the mask part of the helmet) to protect the throat area.

4: HOW TO PLAY LACROSSE

The Basics and Beyond

The objective of the fastest game on two feet is straightforward: Score by shooting the ball into your opponent's goal, and prevent them from shooting the ball into yours. Players move the ball down the field by running and carrying it with their sticks or by passing it to teammates. At the end of the game, the team scoring the most goals wins. Players, with the exception of the goalie, are not allowed to touch the ball with their hands.

Sounds simple enough. And actually, lacrosse is relatively simple to learn to play. But playing really, really well? That's another story.

THE PLAYING FIELD

Field lacrosse is played on grass, on Astroturf, or on other synthetic sport turf. Most players say they prefer to play on a well-groomed grass field, because it's easier on their feet and legs. But since grass is difficult to maintain and many natural fields have uneven terrain, such as holes and bumps, the ideal these days is the next best thing: synthetic turf.

Before a game, the home team designates someone to properly line

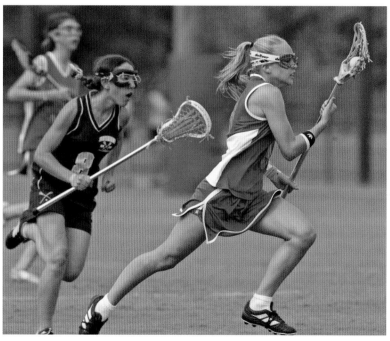

Women hit the field.

the field. Most often, the designee is a coach, referee, or volunteer parent for younger players' teams. The designee, who can also be a

player, field coordinator, or grounds-keeper, uses a field lining machine and cans of noncaustic field paint to line the field. (Make sure to check the rules to learn more about acceptable kinds of paints.) To some degree, the boundaries of outdoor grass fields are determined by natural restrictions; turf fields are obviously more controlled.

Synthetic turf: the next best thing to real grass.

HI-TECH NOTE: As of 2007,

the home team must ensure that direct two-way communication is available at all times between the press box and the scorer's table if official scoring and/or timing functions are not handled at field level.

WOMEN'S FIELDS

Whenever possible, the playing field should measure 120 yards (109.7 m) by 70 yards (64 m). The 2006 rule change states that women's fields also must include solid line boundaries. The total length should be between 110 and 140 yards (100.6–128 m) and total width should be between 60 and 70 yards (54.9–64 meters).

Other designations for marking women's fields, which should be rectangular in shape, include:

- A circle in the center of the field
- Two arcs marked from the center of the goal line

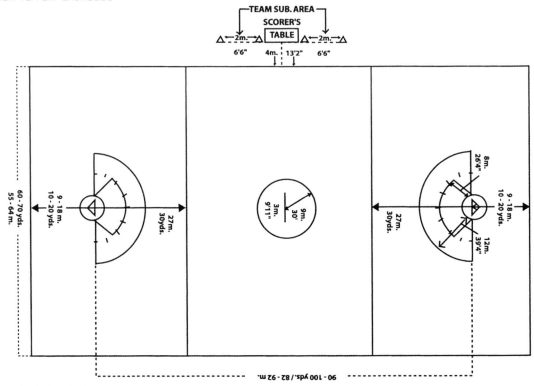

Women's playing field.
Reprinted with permission
of US Lacrosse.

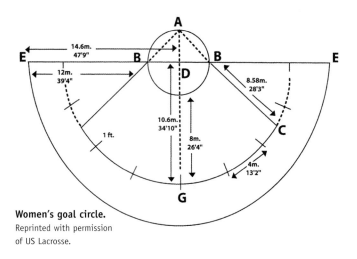

Women's goal circle.
Reprinted with permission
of US Lacrosse.

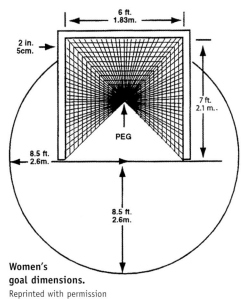

**Women's
goal dimensions.**
Reprinted with permission
of US Lacrosse.

- The 8.75 yard (8 m) bisecting each arc
- 10.97-yard (10-m) fan extending out from the goal line
- A substitution area for each team marked with two cones placed next to and 6 feet, 6 inches (2 m) from the front edge and level with the scorer's table extended.

YOUTH (GIRLS') FIELDS

The field should be marked according to US Lacrosse women's rules. Although youth rules state that officials are free to designate appropriate boundaries, here are some guidelines.

Level A: *Length:* 100 yards (91.4 m)
Width: 70 yards (64 m)
Area behind each goal: 10 yards (9.1 m)

Level B: *Length:* 90 yards (82.3 m)
Width: 50 yards (45.7 m)
Area behind each goal: 10 yards (9.1 m)

Level C: *Length:* 50 yards (45.7 m)
Width: 25 yards (22.9 m)
Area behind each goal: 10 yards (9.1 m)

MEN'S FIELDS

The men's field rules are as follows:

- The playing field is rectangular and measures 110 yards (100.6 m) by 60 yards (54.9 m).

- The boundaries of the field are marked with white or contrasting colored lines.

- The long sides of the field are designated as sidelines; the short sides are designated as end lines.

- The centerline is a bold white or contrasting colored line marked through the center of the field perpendicular to the sidelines.

- All lines should be between 2 and 4 inches (5.1–10.2 cm) wide. The goal must be 2 inches (5.1 cm) wide and the centerline 4 inches (10.2 cm) wide.

BOX NOTES

The box lacrosse indoor "field," often called "the carpet," is an artificial surface, usually Astroturf or another kind of sports turf. Arenas vary in size, as do the fields, but most playing areas feature boards around the sides that are a minimum of 3 feet (0.9 m) high. An average size box field is 200 feet (182.9 m) long and 85 feet (77.7 m) wide.

Boys' lacrosse is a whole different ball game.

YOUTH (BOYS') FIELDS

US Lacrosse suggests that teams play on regulation size fields but coaches and officials are free to designate their own agreed-upon boundaries. Events sponsored by US Lacrosse Youth Council will be played on regulation size fields.

NFHS rules list the following field requirements:

The playing field shall be rectangular, 110 yards [100.6 m] in length and between 53½ and 60 yards [49–54.8 m] in width to accommodate play on existing fields. The boundaries of the field shall be marked with white or contrasting colored lines.

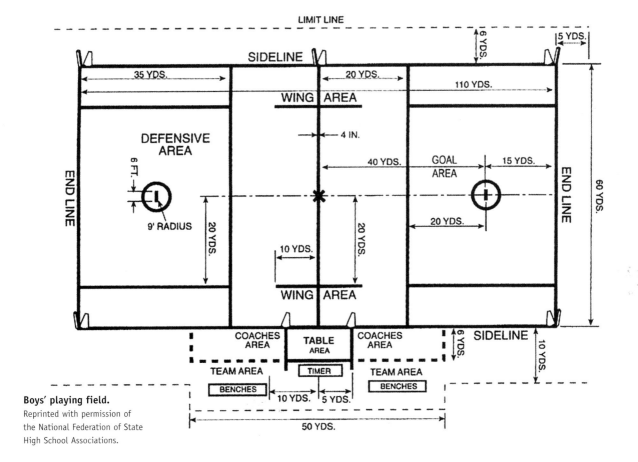

Boys' playing field.
Reprinted with permission of the National Federation of State High School Associations.

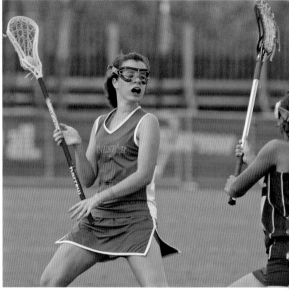

Women play with a 7-inch (17.8-cm) imaginary bubble around their heads.

Ladies First

The biggest news to hit lacrosse in decades was the addition of hard boundaries to the women's game in 2006. In other words, now women have an "out of bounds," whereas previously, they could continue playing an errant ball. In honor of this monumental change, for this section, it's ladies first.

What Are We Doing Here?

According to US Lacrosse rules:

Women's lacrosse is a non-contact game played by 12 players including a goalkeeper, five attackers and six defenders. A goal is scored when the ball passes completely over the goal line and into the goal cage. Scoring must be by an attacker's crosse and not off the body of an attack player. A goal may be scored off the defender's body or crosse.

Let's Play

According to US Lacrosse rules, here is how women play the game:

Start and Stop Women's lacrosse begins with a draw, which is taken by the center position. The ball is placed between two horizontally held crosses (sticks) at the center of the field. At the sound of the whistle, the ball is flung into the air as the crosses are pulled up and away. A draw is used to start each half and after each goal, and it takes place at the center of the field.

[During the game] when a whistle blows, all players must stop in place. When a ball is ruled out of play, the player closest to the ball gets possession when play is resumed. Loss of possession may occur if a player deliberately runs or throws the ball out of play.

Hard boundaries were recently added to the women's game.

Keep It Safe *Rough checks, and contact to the body with the crosse or body, are not allowed, however, incidental body contact may occur.*

Pass and Play *Field players may pass, catch or run with the ball in their crosse. A player may gain possession of the ball by dislodging it from an opponent's crosse with a check. A check is a controlled tap with a crosse on an opponent's crosse in an attempt to knock the ball free. The player must be one step in front of her opponent in order to check. No player may reach across an opponent's body to check the handle of a crosse when she is even with or behind that opponent. A player may not protect the ball in her crosse by cradling so close to her body or face so as to make a legal, safe check impossible for the opponent.*

All legal checks must be directed away from a seven-inch sphere or "bubble" around the head of the player. No player is allowed to touch the

NEW BOUNDARIES

In 2006, hard boundaries were introduced to the women's game. Previously, when a player tossed a ball far "out of bounds" she could retrieve it and continue playing. Although there are some traditionalists who prefer the old rules and need a while to get used to the change, most women players and coaches give the new rules the thumbs up:

Meagan Voight, women's assistant coach, McDaniel College, Westminster, Maryland: "I love the hard boundaries. It makes the game harder; you have to be more skilled. You can't just throw it out of bounds anymore. It's great for defensive players. Now, if you work your butt off to force someone out of bounds you get the ball. A turnover in lacrosse is huge!"

Trish Dabrowski, women's assistant coach, Johns Hopkins, Baltimore, Maryland: "Some older players weren't for it because they didn't want the game to change and move too much towards the men's game. But I love the hard boundaries! You shouldn't get the ball back for a mistake you've made."

Missy Foote, women's head coach, Middlebury College, Vermont: "I like the hard boundaries. I wasn't sure I was going to but I've watched the sport evolve. I started playing in the seventies in college, and thirty-something years later, it's still continuing to evolve. The rules have adapted."

The best teams rely on the passing game.

GAME TIME

WOMEN

College games: 60 minutes long (30 minutes per half)

High school games: 50 minutes long (25 minutes per half)

In college, in high school, and on youth teams following US Lacrosse rules, teams are allowed two timeouts per game, including overtime. As of 2007, "time-outs must be taken anytime the draw must be re-taken." In other words, time-outs may be called after a goal is scored. Not while play is in progress.

YOUTH (GIRLS)

Levels A and B: 50 minutes long (25 minutes per half)

Level C: 40 minutes long (20 minutes per half)

Youth teams may play four quarters instead of two halves, but total playing time must not exceed the maximum time allowed.

ball with her hands except the goalkeeper when she is within the goal circle. A change of possession may occur if a player gains a distinct advantage by playing the ball off her body.

Passing is the fastest way to get the ball down the field. You won't see a game today without plenty of passing. Players receiving a pass strive to catch the ball and immediately gain control by maneuvering the catch into a cradle, the method used to hold the ball in the stick's pocket. She then either passes to a teammate, or if she's close to her opponent's goal, she takes a shot. Then, they do it all again.

When coaches, or refs in the case of a foul, decide a substitution is called for, players may substitute at any time during play, after goals, and at halftime.

Modifications for Girls   For the most part, girls' youth games are played according to women's rules with a few slight modifications, including:

No Check Please!

Girls under the age of 15 should not be stick checking. The reason is young players should be taught fundamentals before they are taught stick checking, which is a more advanced skill. Once coaches feel their players have learned the basics, they may introduce modified stick checking, which is defined as checking the stick when it is below shoulder level, using a downward motion away from the other player's body. As the players mature and gain experience, they can learn regular stick checking. Umpires and coaches should strictly enforce the no checking and modified checking rules for young players, never allowing checks near a player's head or face.

Here are US Lacrosse Rules about stick checking:

Stick-to-stick contact is not necessarily a violation of the no checking/modified checking rule. A defender who is holding her stick in good defensive position may force the attack player to cradle into her stick causing contact. This is not considered a stick check, as the attack player initiated the contact, not the defender. A similar situation would exist when the defender puts her stick up in an attempt to block or intercept a pass and the attacker makes contact while in the act of passing or catching the ball.

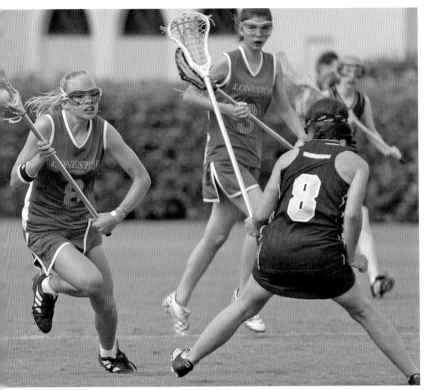

On "D," it's all about the moves.

GUARDING THE GOAL

According to Trish Dabrowski, former Loyola goalkeeper, goalies need to be mentally aggressive. This goes beyond simply not being afraid of the ball. "If a team scores on you two or three times in a row, it's easy to falter," she says. "A great goalie can bounce back from that and learn to separate their mistakes from the mistakes of their teammates. Remember, the ball's got to get through eleven other players to get to you."

Shutouts in lacrosse are virtually nonexistent. A goalie *will* be scored on, and almost always, she will be scored on several times since the game moves so fast.

"It's your job to make the save," says Dabrowski, "but some days it's a beach ball and some days it's a golf ball."

- At the start, for all levels, a free position will be taken at the center by the team with fewer goals if a four or more goal differential exists.
- No checking (Levels B and C).
- Modified checking only (Level A).

WOMEN'S POSITIONS

US Lacrosse rules specify:

Seven attacking players only are allowed over the restraining line in their offensive end and only eight defenders are allowed over the line in their defensive end. The additional defender is the goalkeeper. Players may exchange places during play, but the player should have both feet over the line before the teammate enters.

THE ATTACK: WOMEN'S POSITIONS

Offensive positions including first, second, and third home and the attack wings

POSITION	RESPONSIBILITY	TALENTS
First Home	Scoring	Continually cuts toward the goal to shoot or cuts away to make room for other players. Also displays excellent stick work
Second Home	Playmaking	Shooting well from every angle and distance from the goal
Third Home	Transitioning the ball from defense to attack	Feeding the ball to other players and filling in wing areas
Attack Wings (right and left)	Transitioning the ball from defense to attack	Speed, endurance, and the ability to receive the ball from the defense and run or pass the ball

THE DEFENSE: WOMEN'S POSITIONS

Defensive positions including point, coverpoint, third man, center, defense wings, and the goalie.

POSITION	RESPONSIBILITY	TALENTS
Point	Marking first home	Stick checking, body checking, and intercepting passes
Coverpoint	Marking second home	Receiving clears, running fast, and good footwork
Third Man	Marking third home	Intercepting passes, clearing the ball, running fast, and good footwork
Center	Controlling the draw and playing both defense and attack	Speed and endurance
Defense Wings	Marking the attack wings and bringing the ball into the attack area	Speed and endurance
Goalkeeper	Protecting the goal and preventing opponent from scoring	Excellent stick work, courage, confidence, and supreme bravery

Most lacrosse players, particularly at the youth and high school levels, play several different positions during a season. In college, especially at schools with excellent teams, players also tend to play more than one position. There are a number of reasons for this, including versatility—a team wants to be adaptable—and reality—if six freshmen played center in high school, they can't all play center on their new college team.

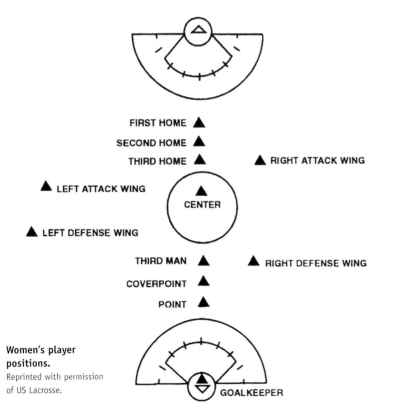

FIRST HOME ▲
SECOND HOME ▲
THIRD HOME ▲   ▲ RIGHT ATTACK WING

▲ LEFT ATTACK WING   ▲
                        CENTER

▲ LEFT DEFENSE WING

THIRD MAN ▲   ▲ RIGHT DEFENSE WING
COVERPOINT ▲
POINT ▲

▲ GOALKEEPER

Women's player positions.
Reprinted with permission of US Lacrosse.

"AIR-GAIT"

With all this talk about the dos and don'ts of lacrosse, it's easy to forget that when you're playing, it's much more about doing than thinking. Spontaneity takes over. Take, for instance, the most famous play ever made in lacrosse. In 1988, Gary Gait, playing for Syracuse against Penn in the national semifinal, leapt from outside the crease behind the goal and dunked a shot around front for the score. The incredible shot—unbelievably, he repeated it during the game—has been known ever since as "Air-Gait." Syracuse won 11–10.

GIRLS' YOUTH SPECS AT-A-GLANCE

	LEVEL A	LEVEL B	LEVEL C
Number of players	11 field players; 1 goalkeeper	11 field players; 1 goalkeeper	7 field players; 1 goalkeeper optional
Recommended field size	100 yards (91.4 m) long by 70 yards (64 m) wide	90 yards (82.3 m) long by 50 yards (45.7 m) wide	50 yards (45.7 m) long by 25 yards (22.9 m) wide
Field markings	Regular, including restraining line	Regular, including restraining line	26.3-foot (8-m) arc, no 39½-foot (12-m) fan, no restraining line, centerline with no circle.
Crosse specs	Regular women's crosse with regulation pockets	Regular women's crosse with modified pockets	Youth sticks (mesh allowed) or regular women's crosse with modified pockets
Checking	Modified checking only	No checking allowed	No checking allowed
Game time	50 minutes long (25 minutes per half)	50 minutes long (25 minutes per half)	40 minutes long (20 minutes per half)
Shooting from free positions	Allowed	Allowed	Not allowed

BOX PLAYERS

Box lacrosse is played with six players. A group of five players make up the line: two creasemen (right and left), two cornermen (right and left), and a pointman. On the transition from defense to offense, the pointman runs up the side or middle of the floor. And don't forget the goalie.

BOYS' VS. GIRLS' LAX AT-A-GLANCE

	BOYS	GIRLS
Number of players	10	12
Recommended field size	110 yards (100.6 m) long by 60 yards (54.9 m) wide	100 yards (91.4 m) long by 70 yards (64 m) wide
Contact	Contact allowed	Contact *not* allowed
Checking	Checking allowed, but no body checking at lower youth levels	No checking at youth levels; modified and stick checking only for high school levels and above
Bubble rule	No	Yes. Sticks are not allowed to enter an imaginary 7-inch (17.8-cm) bubble around any player's head
Protective equipment	Yes	Minimal. Only goalies wear extensive protective equipment and helmets. Other players wear goggles and mouth guards
Crosse	Large, wide crosse with deep pocket	Narrow crosse with shallow pocket; level C girls can use youth crosse
Game start	Face-off	Draw
Field markings	Midfield line restricts the number of players who may cross over to six attackers and seven defenders in the scoring area	Restraining line allows seven attackers and eight defenders in the scoring area
Penalties	30-second suspension; opposing team gains possession of the ball	Free position shot
Ref's calls	Ref's whistle signifies a call being made, although all players don't immediately stop	Ref's whistle means all players must stand

THE GUYS HAVE IT

Boys' lacrosse is considered very rugged—plenty of hitting, stick on stick combat, and fast-moving balls—and very cool, chock full of stick tricks, leaping throws, and dramatic saves. But, before a player graduates to the most impressive moves, he needs to learn the ins and outs of the game.

WHAT ARE WE DOING HERE?

According to US Lacrosse:

Boys lacrosse is a contact game played by ten players: a goalie, three defensemen, three midfielders and three attackmen. The object of the game is to shoot the ball into the opponent's goal and to keep the other team from scoring. The team scoring the most goals wins.

LET'S PLAY

First comes the coin toss. The winning team chooses the goal it would like to defend first. (Teams switch sides every quarter.) Next, players take their positions on the field, four in the defensive area, one at center, two in the wings, and three in their attack goal area.

Next, according to US Lacrosse rules:

The Start *Men's lacrosse begins with a face-off. The ball is placed between the sticks of two squatting players at the center of the field. The official*

GAME TIME

MEN

College games: 60 minutes long (four 15-minute quarters)

High school games: 48 minutes long (four 12-minute quarters)

YOUTH (BOYS)

Senior and Junior divisions: Four quarters, 10-minute stop clock, and sudden victory 4-minute overtime periods are used

Lightning and Bantam divisions: Four quarters, 12-minute running clock, and a 5-minute overtime running clock; no sudden victory

In the event of a tie in Senior and Junior divisions, two 4-minute (sudden victory) overtime periods will be played. If, after two overtime periods the score is tied, additional sudden victory overtime periods may be played until a winner is determined, providing time permits and coaches and officials are in agreement. Two timeouts are permitted per half.

The guys play
a rugged game.

blows the whistle to begin play. Each face-off player tries to control the ball. The players in the wing areas can run after the ball when the whistle sounds. The other players must wait until one player has gained possession of the ball, or the ball has crossed a goal area line, before they can release.

Restart Center face-offs are also used at the start of each quarter and after a goal is scored.

Watch out for midfielders, who may roam the entire length of the field.

Stick with It Field players must use their crosses to pass, catch, and run with the ball. Only the goalkeeper may touch the ball with his hands.

Check Please A player may gain possession of the ball by dislodging it from an opponent's crosse with a stick check, which is the controlled poking and slapping of the stick and gloved hands of the player in possession of the ball.

Body checking is permitted if the opponent has the ball or is within five yards of a loose ball. All body contact must occur from the front or the side, above the waist and below the shoulders and with both hands on the stick. An opponent's crosse may be stick checked if it is within five yards of a loose ball or ball in the air. Aggressive body checking is discouraged.

On the Field If the ball or a player in possession of the ball goes out of bounds, the other team is awarded possession. If the ball goes out of bounds after an unsuccessful shot, the player nearest to the ball when and where it goes out of bounds is awarded possession.

An attacking player cannot enter the crease around the goal, but may reach in with his stick to scoop a loose ball.

MEN'S POSITIONS

POSITION	RESPONSIBILITY	TALENTS
Attackmen (3 players)	Scoring goals and helping teammates score goals by passing the ball. Generally restricts play to the offensive end of the field.	Excellent stick work with both hands and quick feet to maneuver around the goal.
Midfielder (3 players)	Covering the entire field, playing both offense and defense. The key to the transition game, often called upon to clear the ball from defense to offense.	Speed and stamina. Good stick work including throwing, catching, and scooping.
Defensemen or Close Defense (3 players)	Defending the goal. Generally restricted to the defensive end of the field.	Reacts quickly in game situations. Great stick work plus agility and aggressiveness.
Goalkeeper	Protecting the goal to prevent the other team from scoring.	Excellent hand-eye coordination, a strong voice, speed, agility, confidence, ability to concentrate, and supreme bravery.

The US Lacrosse Youth Council has adopted modified rules for play by youth ages 15 and under. For example, it is suggested that teams be made up of ten players on a side, but games may be played with as few as seven on a side if all coaches agree.

Also, in any game where a four-point lead exists, the trailing team will be given the ball at the midfield line in lieu of a face-off. These rules are offered as modifications to the NFHS rules and may be found in full at uslacrosse.org.

BOYS' POSITIONS

US Lacrosse states:

Each team must keep at least four players, including the goalie, in its defensive half of the field and three in its offensive half. Three players (mid-fielders) may roam the entire field.

ALL PLAYERS

Attack: The offensive team.

Backdoor cut: A cut in which an attacker cuts behind the defender toward the goal or ball.

Back-up: An attacker's move into a position to regain possession after a shot. Also refers to an off-ball defender in position to support a teammate guarding the ball carrier.

Catching: The act of receiving a passed ball with the crosse.

Channel: When a defender forces her opponent to veer in one direction and maintain that path.

Check-up: A call given by the goalie to tell each defender to find his man and call out his number.

Clearing: Any action taken by a player within the goal circle to pass or carry the ball out of the goal circle.

Cutting: Movement by a player without the ball in anticipation of a pass.

Decoy cut: A cut intended to move the defender out of a space and not necessarily to receive a pass.

Defense: The team not in possession of the ball.

Deputy: A player who enters the goal circle when the goalie is not there and his or her team is in possession of the ball.

Dodging: The act of suddenly shifting direction in order to avoid an opponent.

Drop down: A defender's move away from his or her player and toward the goal area to help defend a second player.

Fast-break: A transition scoring opportunity in which the offense has at least a one-man advantage.

Feeding: Passing the ball to a teammate who is in position for a shot on goal.

Goal line: Line painted on the field between the two goalposts over which the ball must pass entirely for a team to score a goal.

Ground ball: A loose ball on the playing field.

Grounded: Refers to any part of the goalkeeper's or deputy's body touching the ground for support outside of the goal circle when he or she attempts to play the ball from inside the goal circle.

Hole: The area immediately outside of the crease in front of the goal.

Invert: Isolating oneself by carrying the ball in front of the goal (attackers) or behind the goal (midfielders).

Isolation: The space created by a ball carrier and his teammates so he may dodge an opponent in a one-on-one situation.

Go girls!

Marking: Being within a stick's length of an opponent. It's also often said that a player at this distance is being "closely guarded."

Off-ball movement: Cuts and movement by players without the ball that cause the defense to relocate.

Offense: The team in possession of the ball.

Open player: An offensive team member who is not marked and does not possess the ball.

Passing: The act of throwing the ball to a teammate with the crosse.

Passing lane: The aerial space between the ball carrier and her teammate's stick through which a pass will travel if it is made.

Player to player: A strategy where each defender closely marks an opponent and remains with him or her throughout the play.

Possession: When a player has the ball in his or her crosse.

Riding: The act of trying to prevent a team from clearing the ball.

Rolling the crease: A move around the goal circle by an attacker with the ball who attempts to cut off her defender and takes a shot on goal from close range.

Scooping (or pick-ups): The act of retrieving or scooping a loose ground ball with a crosse.

Scoring play: A continuous effort by the attacking team to move the ball toward the goal and to complete a shot on goal.

Screening: An offensive tactic in which a player near the crease positions himself so as to block the goalkeeper's view of the ball.

Shooting: The act of throwing the ball at the goal with the crosse in an attempt to score.

Slide: A move by a defender to leave one player to mark a more dangerous opponent.

Unsettled situation: Any situation in which the defense is not positioned correctly, usually due to a loose ball or broken clear.

WOMEN

Checking (or crosse checking): The act of using a controlled tap, or a series of sharp, controlled taps, with a crosse on an opponent's crosse in an attempt to dislodge the ball.

Cradling: The act of moving the stick from side to side, causing the ball to remain in the upper part of the pocket webbing.

Critical scoring area: An area 49.2 feet (15 m) in front of and to each side of the goal and 29.5 feet (9 m) behind the goal. An 26.3-foot (8-m) arc and 39.4-foot (12-m) fan are marked in the area.

Draw: A technique to start or resume play. The ball is placed in between the sticks of two standing players and drawn up and away.

Free space to goal: A cone-shaped path from each side of the goal circle to the attack player with the ball. A defense player may not, for safety reasons, stand alone in this area without closely marking an opponent.

Goal circle (or crease): The circle around the goal with a radius of 8.5 feet (2.6 m).

Modified checking (youth rules): Checking the stick only if it is below shoulder level. The check must be in a downward direction and away from the body.

Position to check (youth rules): Player has an opportunity to legally check the stick without fouling. The 3-second count starts when the umpire deems that the player with the ball could be checked legally if checking were permitted.

Weak-side defender: A defensive teammate who is not on the ball side of the field.

MEN

Attack goal area: The area around the goal defined by the end line, the goal area line, and the two broken lines located 20 yards (18.3 m) on either side of the goal. Once the offensive team crosses the midfield line, it has 10 seconds to move the ball into its attack goal area.

Body check: Contact with an opponent from the front—between the shoulders and waist—when the opponent has the ball or is within 5 yards (4.6 m) of a loose ball. At no time should a player initiate or receive body contact with his head.

Checking: The act of attempting to dislodge the ball from an opponent's stick.

Clamp: A face-off maneuver executed by quickly pushing the back of the stick on top of the ball.

Cradling: The coordinated motion of the arms and wrists that keeps the ball secure in the pocket and ready to be passed or shot when running.

Crease: A circle around the goal with a radius of 9 feet (2.7 m) into which only defensive players may enter. Defensive players may not take the ball into the crease.

Defensive clearing area: The area defined by a line drawn sideline to sideline, 20 yards (18.3 m) from the face of the goal. Once the defensive team gains possession of the ball in this area, it has 10 seconds to move the ball beyond the goal area line. Once beyond the goal area line, the defensive team may not pass or run the ball back into the defensive clearing area.

Face-off: A technique used to put the ball in play at the start of each quarter, or after a goal is scored. The players squat down, and the ball is placed between their crosses.

Goal line extended: An imaginary line that runs parallel to the end line from the goalposts to the sideline.

Man-ball: Where one player scoops a loose ball while a teammate checks the opponent close to the ball [within a legal 5-yard (4.6-m) distance].

Midfield line: The line bisecting the field of play.

On-the-fly substitution: A substitution made during play while the clock is running.

Pick: An offensive maneuver in which a stationary player attempts to block the path of a defender guarding another offensive player.

5: PRACTICE MAKES PERFECT

Drills, Thrills, and Stick Skills

Lacrosse players do a lot of running. From quick starts and explosive sprints to endurance runs across the field, the pace and intensity of the game requires a high level of cardiovascular fitness.

How do you get in shape for all that running? Train hard—all year round. During game season and especially in off-season months, lax players hit the gym regularly to focus on strength training while keeping up with challenging cardio routines. Coaches also encourage players to try other sports—football, hockey, running, bicycling, swimming, cross-country skiing—during summer and winter months. A new sport means new skills, and these new skills can give players an edge when Fall Ball is back in session.

And, don't forget: A crosse is a lacrosse player's best friend. Practice makes perfect when it comes to stick tricks, so work on them all year long. Do the drills. And then do them again.

GET READY

So, you want to play lacrosse? If it's summer, and Fall Ball is months away, there are still plenty of ways to get busy preparing for the season ahead and, more importantly, log some playing time.

LAX CAMPS

Lacrosse is booming and so are the opportunities to attend summer clinics and camps all over the country. There are camps of every stripe for everyone from beginners to national team hopefuls. Some camps last for a day, some last for a week, so gauge your desire and look into one that best suits your needs. Camps are a great place to learn and hone basic skills and to make friends who also love the game. Camps are also a terrific place for more experienced players to work on specific skills or positions; for example, there are camps just for goalies.

US Lacrosse and *Lacrosse Magazine* are great sources for camps. It's best to start researching camps in the early spring since many of the more popular ones, featuring well-known coaches from top-notch programs, fill up fast.

> "There's a high learning curve for lacrosse. But when you get it, you really get it."
>
> —COACH MISSY FOOTE

Camp out: The off-season is a great time to learn or hone your skills.

STICK WITH IT

When a player gets a new stick, she'll want to get comfortable with it right away. Coaches always say, "Your stick is an extension of yourself." So how do you go about making your stick a natural and comfortable part of your body? Hold it. Play around with it. Restring it. And most importantly, get outside and throw and catch with it. You may also want to try holding your stick and cradling the ball while looking in the mirror. At first, the idea is to simply get used to your stick. Don't worry about rules or trying complicated moves in the beginning. And don't forget—it's important to learn to hold the stick in both hands.

Missy Foote, women's coach at Middlebury College in Vermont, strongly encourages parents to throw with their kids: "Throwing and catching are skills that are easily learned. Get out and try it. You'll learn the mechanics of the sport. Plus, you'll gain a connection between what you're learning and what your daughter is learning."

"The more you practice passing the better. Passing turns into shooting, and shooting turns into winning lacrosse." —JEFF TAMBRONI, HEAD COACH, CORNELL UNIVERSITY

OFF THE WALL

One of the great things about lacrosse is that you can practice with or without a partner. As long as you have a wall.

Lacrosse players call it "Wall Ball," and it's an excellent way to practice catching, throwing, and stick handling before, during, and after lacrosse season. Throwing against the wall gives players more opportunities to make contact with the ball—lax players call these "touches"—than they'd get in a regular practice. Soon, players will notice improved accuracy and focus. This includes goalies!

Step one:
Find a wall.
Step two:
Throw and catch.
Throw and catch.
Repeat.

Remember, in Wall Ball, the ball comes back to you quicker than a partner can throw it, so get ready. Here's what you do:

1. Find a big wall, preferably a brick one with no windows!
2. Stand 5 to 10 yards (4.6–9.2 m) away from the wall.

3. Throw the ball at the wall, and catch it as it bounces back to you.

4. Vary your throws. Go high. Go low. Switch hands.

5. Try catching the ball behind your back.

6. Add motion by throwing as you move slowly down the wall.

The best part of playing Wall Ball, besides the fact that it's fun and you can do it alone, is that most players catch on very quickly. You'll have immediate success, and that will translate into confidence on the field.

TIPS AND DRILLS

■ Chalk some X's on various points on the wall. Dip your ball in water so the ball will leave a mark when you shoot. This is a great way to check your accuracy!

■ If it's cold or rainy outside or if you don't have access to a wall, consider buying a bounceback or a lacrosse shooter to put in your basement. This piece of equipment automatically returns the ball back to you. Or, some inventive players even practice indoors by shooting a tennis ball into a beanbag chair. Anything to keep that stick in your hands and moving.

■ Try playing Wall Ball with your team—move down the line, then back again as a unit.

STICK TRICKS

From the first time a player picks up a stick, he has the uncontrollable urge to spin it, whip it, twirl it, and toss it, with or without the ball in the pocket. This urge leads players to begin practicing stick tricks— cool moves that are fun to do and actually help a lacrosse player improve his game.

Although many of the coolest stick tricks are not actually utilized during a game—you won't see many youth players flipping their stick behind their back while running down the field—learning these moves makes players more comfortable with their sticks. And that's every player's goal.

Trish Dabrowski, Johns Hopkins women's assistant coach and former Loyola goalkeeper, is known for her impressive stick tricks. She has said, "Whenever the stick's in my hand, I'm always playing with it. . . . I'm always trying to come up with something new and creative."

One of Dabrowski's favorite tricks is the "Tiger Woods." She tosses her stick in the air and hits it off one sidewall, and then off the other, as many times as she can before catching it again. Another favorite: the as-yet-unnamed move where she tosses the stick behind her back, flips the shaft straight up, then catches it in front.

The off-season is an excellent time to learn and practice stick tricks, which are a staple at youth camps. Coaches or other players are a great source for learning tricks. So is the Internet, which features demonstrations on several sites including mikeypowell.com and the British Columbia Lacrosse Association Web site, bclacrosse.com.

STICK TRICK TIPS

- Learn as many tricks as you can.
- Try to make up your own tricks.
- Learn to do every trick with both hands.
- Practice doing stickies with and without the ball.
- Use stick tricks as a warm-up before practice, or practice them during down time, for example, when you're waiting for a ride.

STICKIES

There are dozens of stick tricks (a.k.a. "stickies") and dozens more not yet invented. Here are some popular ones:

Forward bump (basic): Hold the stick in one hand with the ball in the pocket. Extend it straight in front of you, parallel to the ground, and toss the ball straight up. While the ball is in the air, flip the stick over, and bump the ball back up in the air with the stick. Flip the shaft back over, and catch the ball.

Helicopter (basic): With the ball in the pocket, lift the stick up parallel to the ground, extended in front of you. Pop the ball straight up in the air, then turn the stick halfway around (like a helicopter blade) and catch the ball.

Back breaker (challenging): Start with feet apart. Hold the stick in both hands, and extend it in front of you so it touches the ground. Put the ball in the pocket. Slowly lift the stick above and then behind your head, and let it drop between your legs as you shoot the ball in front of you.

Hidden ball trick (a.k.a. the ice-cone play): This one can be used during a game. The player fakes flipping the ball to her teammate and instead hangs on to the ball.

Cardio Training

Although many college and club teams play on fall schedules, spring is the primary season for lacrosse. Many lax coaches encourage their players to play other sports during summer and winter, their team's off-season. This kind of cross training not only helps players cultivate new skills but also keeps them in shape.

No question about it: Lacrosse players put in the miles.

WHAT'S CARDIO?

Lacrosse players run constantly in short bursts and for long stretches across the length of the field. For this reason, athletes must be in good cardio shape. "Cardio" means heart. So when you "do cardio" you are improving your heart's ability to function and pump fresh blood to your muscles as you run. You are also strengthening your respiratory system, which is why you don't get out of breath as easily when you're in shape.

Endurance athletes, such as lacrosse players, should aim to train in their aerobic zone, the stage of a workout where the body utilizes stored oxygen, at 70 to 80 percent of the maximum heart rate. To calculate your maximum heart rate, subtract your age from 220. Then calculate 70 to 80 percent of that number to get your zone.

The following calculation is for a 16-year-old:

Max heart rate: 220 – 16 = 204

80 percent of 204 = 163

70 percent of 204 = 142

So a 16-year-old should aim for a heart rate between 142 and 163 during her workout. If you don't have a stopwatch or clock to calculate an accurate heart rate, a good indicator that you are training in your desired aerobic zone is when you can't easily carry on a conversation but you are not yet out of breath.

The first day of practice is no time to begin getting in shape. Today's athlete, whether he is an Olympic hopeful or a freshman hoping to make the varsity, shows up *game ready* at the start of the season. That way, he can focus on learning new skills and meshing with his team instead of trying to run 20 yards (18 m) without having to stop and rest. Many college and high school coaches provide information to their players, usually in the form of handouts, about what they should do during the off-season to stay in shape and even improve some skills during the down time.

Since lacrosse players run—and run a lot—a player's primary off-season goal should be to maintain cardiovascular strength. Running, bicycling, kickboxing, swimming, and in-line skating during the summer and cross-country skiing or playing hockey in the winter are all excellent ways to train. Playing soccer, football, or basketball, and ideally a combination of all three, also provides a well-balanced cardio workout.

WEIGHT TRAINING

The off-season is also a chance to increase strength, and many coaches outline a weight training routine to complement a player's cardio training. Remember: Every athlete is different, so it's best to consult with a trainer or your coach to create an individual plan, especially if you have not previously worked out with weights. There are also many excellent books to consult, such as *Supertraining* by Mel Siff, and periodicals, such as *The Strength and Conditioning Journal* published by the National Strength and Conditioning Association.

Brian Yeager, head strength and conditioning coach for the pro lax team the Philadelphia Barrage, has said, "Train hard or go home."

In general, to develop maximum strength an athlete should plan on four days of weight training a week (two days of upper body and two days of lower body). These workouts are often combined with cardio by lifting weights first, then going for a run or swim. Many athletes today also practice circuit training, a highly time-efficient gym workout where coaches combine an aerobic workout and weight work at the same time by moving quickly from machine to machine without resting. Circuit training is usually done when endurance is being emphasized over strength.

Here are a few basic weight-training exercises you can do at home with free weights and a bench. Remember, in order to increase your strength, you'll want to lift slightly heavier weights for fewer reps. Try to pick a weight you can lift slowly up to eight or nine times.

Bench Press *(works the chest)* Lie on your back on a bench. Your feet should be flat on the floor. Grasp the barbell (or two free weights) from the rack with your hands shoulder width apart. Slowly lower the barbell to just above your chest, then raise it straight up and extend your arms fully. Repeat.

Military Press *(works the shoulders)* Sit up on the end of the bench or stand up straight. Pick up the barbell (or two free weights) and bring it to shoulder level with your elbows down by your sides. Lift the weight directly over your head, hold, then lower and return to the starting position. Repeat.

Bicep Curl *(works the biceps)* Sit up on the end of the bench or stand up straight. Hold the barbell (or two free weights) with an underhand grip, resting gently on top of your thighs. Bend your elbows, and lift the bar slowly up to your chest. Slowly lower the barbell, keeping arms in line with your shoulders. Repeat.

Squats *(works the quads and glutes)* Stand up straight. With your arms down by your sides, hold a free weight in each hand. Step backward with your right leg, bending both legs but dropping your right thigh parallel to the floor. Keep your arms at your sides. Return to the starting position, and repeat on the left side.

Sit-Ups *(works the abs)* Lie on your back, knees bent, with your hands behind your head and your elbows extended out to the side. Slowly lift your shoulder blades off the floor, and come up as far as you can without lifting your lower back off the floor. Hold and return to the starting position. Repeat.

WEIGHT TRAINING TIPS

- Try to work up to doing three sets of each exercise.
- Make your movements slow and controlled.
- Start with the largest muscles first, and target smallest muscles last.
- Try doing strength before cardio so you don't tire as easily.
- Remember to breathe. It's hard to work the muscles while holding your breath.

Year-Round

Lacrosse players work hard all year-round, especially during their main spring playing season. It's easy to motivate a team on game day, when their adrenaline is pumping. But how do coaches keep players from getting bored and burning out the rest of the time? Chris Endlich, the strength and conditioning coach for women's lacrosse at Johns Hopkins University and boys' lacrosse at Calvert Hall, says the key to motivation is variety. "We do so many different things," Endlich said. "No two days are ever alike."

> "Lacrosse is a great sport that can be your best friend for a very long time." —DOM STARSIA, HEAD COACH, UNIVERSITY OF VIRGINIA

At Hopkins, Endlich peppers the training program with fun, alternative workouts, such as kickboxing and swimming. He also makes it a point to utilize a variety of strength training equipment, such as stability balls and resistance bands.

High school players also train hard. Years ago, athletes under the age of 18 just hit the field and played. Not so anymore. Many youth programs, especially those at well-funded private schools, have a full- or part-time strength and conditioning coach on hand to supervise training. Brian Yeager, strength and conditioning coach for the Philadelphia Barrage and owner of Pro Strength, also works with

Get warm. Then get to work.

several youth programs, including Villa Maria Academy for Girls in Malvern, Pennsylvania. "I started out working with girls," Yeager said. "I learned that they wanted to increase their strength and conditioning to become better players, just like the guys did."

So, Yeager gets his girls and boys in the gym regularly to hit the weight machines. But he also incorporates seriously unique workouts on the field, such as sled dragging (where players pull a large weight after attaching themselves to it with a rope and belt) and tire flipping, a favorite among young players.

Tire flipping is a strongman exercise (think the big, muscle-bound guys on ESPN) and an excellent way to develop explosive strength, a lax player's best friend. Yeager finds old truck tires and hauls them to the field. "Companies have to pay to have these taken away so they're

FIT GOALIES

Don't forget the goalie!

Like every lacrosse player, goalies need to have excellent endurance. Goalkeepers may work on this throughout the season and off-season by regularly (2–3 times a week) running long distances of 2 miles (3.2 km) or more. But goalies need explosive power, which is acquired through strength training and conditioning. Goalies should focus on short sprints and plenty of footwork to improve their lateral motion.

◦ Use the 26.3-foot (8-m) mark as a reference, and do sets of short sprints up to the dash. Try doing 10 with a short rest in between.

◦ Run the ladder, side to side through tires or an imaginary ladder.

◦ Jump rope. Go as fast as you can for 2 minutes. Rest. Then go again. Vary footwork between one foot, two feet, and skipping.

happy to give them to you," he said. Players focus on trying to drive through the tire explosively, rather than trying to deadlift it.

How exactly do you flip a tire? Start by standing about 1 foot (30 cm) away from a tire lying on its side. Grip the tire, and press your chest against it with your chin resting on top. Imagine driving the tire up and forward at a forty-five-degree angle while your shoulders and hips rise at the same time.

To build strength, use heavier tires and perform a high number of sets for low repetitions. To improve strength endurance, use a smaller tire and go for distance or time.

Yeager has developed a specific training template for high school players. For the full program, please see the Appendix.

GET WARM

Every player, including the goalie, needs to warm up before practice or play. Most teams begin by jogging a lap or two around the field. Next, they line up for stretches, beginning with motion or dynamic stretches, where players move as they stretch. Examples include:

Russian kicks: High leg kicks to stretch the hamstrings

Butt kicks: Players kick their butts as they jog to stretch their quads

High knees: Knee raises to stretch hip flexors and glutes

After this dynamic routine, players begin line drills to complete their warm-up. Here is a sample short dynamic warm-up from Chris Endlich, Johns Hopkins strength and conditioning coach:

Do each of the following moves for 5 to 10 seconds, then repeat the entire sequence three times.

1. *Standing twists*
2. *Lateral squats, alternating sides*
3. *Feet in, groin stretch (frog)*
4. *Grab toes and straighten legs*
5. *Walk hands out, stretch abs*
6. *Hips up, stretch calves*
7. *Lunge step right leg, right elbow to ground*
8. *Grab right toes, lift hips, straighten leg*
9. *Kneel on left leg, and grab left foot to stretch quad (you can stretch the quads after you stand up instead)*
10. *Drop right leg back, and walk feet forward to stretch hamstrings*
11. *Walk feet back, drop hips to stretch abs*
12. *Lift hips and stretch calves*
13. *Lunge step left leg, left elbow to ground*
14. *Grab left toes, lift hips, straighten leg*
15. *Kneel on right leg, and grab right foot to stretch quad*
16. *Drop left leg back, and walk hands back, then stand up*

The frog.

Do static stretches after warming up or after practice.

Stretch!

Stretching is an important part of training, during the season and off-season. According to the American College of Sports Medicine, if done regularly and carefully, stretching can increase range of motion in the joints and contribute to improved athletic performance, nourish muscle tissue, and improve coordination and posture. That said, the current school of thought discourages stretching cold muscles. In other words, never start your workout by stretching. Only do it after a warm-up or ideally after a full workout.

Motion, or dynamic stretching, as described above, may be performed in the beginning of a workout after a brief warm-up. Static, or stationary, stretching, where the athlete holds the stretch, should be done later in the workout.

Although for years, coaches and athletes believed stretching could prevent injury, there have been no conclusive studies published to prove this. On the plus side, most trainers believe stretching may help an athlete recover from an injury more quickly. For a more detailed explanation of stretching, including diagrams of sample stretches, two good sources are the *American Council on Exercise Personal Trainer's Manual* and *Stretching*, by Bob Anderson.

Here is a sample post-workout stretch routine, and a few tips, from Chris Endlich, Johns Hopkins strength and conditioning coach:

After every workout, both lifting and conditioning, you need to perform the following routine. Do not rush through it because a flexible body moves much more efficiently and effectively then a tight body. Hold each stretch for about 20 seconds. The total routine should take about 10 minutes.

From a standing position:

1. *Legs out wide, stretch to the middle*
2. *Move your upper body toward the right foot*
3. *Move your upper body toward the left foot*
4. *Stagger your feet so that you are in a lunge with your right foot forward; bend your right knee keeping your left leg straight until you feel a stretch in your left hip flexor*
5. *With your right hand on your right hip, reach your left hand up as high as you can over your head, then lean toward your right, bending at the hip*
6. *Switch your feet and arms to stretch the other sides*
7. *Grab a pole with both hands; bend at your waist, and stretch the sides of your upper body*
8. *In a doorway or corner, place your hands on the sides of the doorway or wall, and lean forward to stretch the front of your upper body*
9. *Finally, stretch your calves on a step or slanted board*

Stretching may help prevent injuries.

STRETCHING TIPS

- Only stretch when the body is warmed up.

- Never bounce while stretching.

- Stretch until muscles feel tight but before you feel pain.

- Hold stretches for 10 to 30 seconds.

- Don't hold your breath while stretching. Take deep, full breaths.

- Stretch as often as possible, ideally every day.

Stretch it out.

From a seated position:

1. Legs out wide, stretch to the middle

2. Legs out wide, stretch toward the right foot

3. Legs out wide, stretch toward the left foot

4. Repeat each of the first three stretches

5. Perform a butterfly. Bring the bottom of your feet together, keep your back straight, and hold onto the ankles (not the feet); push down on your thighs with your elbows

Lying on your back:

1. Pull right knee into the chest, hugging the leg

2. Straighten the right leg for a hamstring stretch

3. Take the right leg across your body for a lower back and glute stretch; make sure to keep both shoulders on the ground

4. Roll onto your left side; pull your right foot toward your back to stretch your quad

5. Repeat for the left leg

You should also spend extra time on the areas that are the tightest.

Get in position.

IT'S UNIVERSAL

Trainers and coaches may have heard of something called the "universal sports position." The most successful athletes in every sport, from golf to skating to football, strike a pose at a key point in their movement where they are semi-crouched on the balls of their feet, with hands in front, and their torso centered over the lower body.

Basically, they are balanced and ready to spring into motion. This position is perfect for lacrosse players, especially defensemen, who perform many explosive movements (cutting, dodging, faking). So, if you want to boost acceleration, agility, and your vertical leap, get your torso in line.

Of course lacrosse players need to assume this position with their stick in hand. So to begin, a player should hold his stick parallel to the ground with his arms at his sides. Hands are hip-width apart. The palm of his top hand faces forward, and his bottom hand grasps the butt of the stick with that palm facing his body. He then raises the stick to his shoulder on the same side as his dominant hand.

Now, he's ready.

FEED ME

Food is fuel for athletes. A lacrosse player who doesn't consume enough calories soon finds himself running out of steam whether he's in the gym or running down the field.

There have quite possibly been more books, not to mention newspaper and magazine articles, written about general diet and nutrition than any other topic. Many of these sources have information that per-

As little as 3 percent dehydration in your body can cause a 10 percent drop in performance, so drink plenty of water!

tains to athletes pursuing endurance sports such as lacrosse. One excellent resource is *The Sports Nutrition Guidebook*, Third Edition, 2003, by Nancy Clark. This book has information for athletes to determine their own best individual nutritional plan.

Despite the current low-carb trend, it's important for athletes to remember that they rely on carbohydrates for performance, especially wholesome, complex carbohydrates, such as those found in multi-grain bread or oatmeal. Athletes need to maximize glycogen (carbohydrate) stores for both training and competition.

Protein is an important part of the diet, but athletes will find that too much protein may hinder their performance since the body digests proteins relatively slowly. (Therefore, it's especially important to avoid too much protein right before a game.)

In addition to eating a well-balanced diet, the best thing a player can do to enhance her performance and keep from feeling fatigued is to drink water. Hydration is extremely important, especially on game day. An athlete should remember to drink water throughout the day leading up to a game as well as the day before a game or a practice. If he waits to hydrate while playing, it may be too late. To give a specific number, the National Athletic Trainers' Association (NATA) recommends drinking approximately 16 to 20 ounces (0.5–0.6 L) of fluids about two hours before working out.

NUTRITION TIPS

- Small, frequent meals are best to help avoid energy dips caused by low blood sugar.
- Each meal should consist of a lean protein (chicken, tuna, tofu), fibrous carbohydrate (lettuce, cauliflower, cucumber), and healthy fats (olive oil, nuts, fish).
- Avoid high-fat and high-sugar snacks and meals. These can slow you down faster than a tough defender.
- Try to get your vitamins from real food as opposed to supplements. Protein, minerals, fiber, and energy are best utilized by the body when provided by actual calories.
- On workout days, aim to consume plenty of water, at least half your body weight in ounces (milliliters, ml).
- Carbo-load throughout the week before a game and for the first four hours afterward for optimum recovery.
- Don't overeat late the night before a game. Also, try to eat a light breakfast the morning before a game or practice.
- During a workout or game you are burning what you ate and stored 24 to 48 hours earlier.
- Experiment with diet and hydration during practice—but not on game day!

SKILLS AND DRILLS

At every practice, players spend a great deal of time doing drills. The very word, "drill," may make some athletes shudder—picture a drill sergeant yelling, "Get down and give me twenty!" But lacrosse drills are usually a lot of fun, especially if the coach designs them to move fast and provide players with multiple chances to be in contact with the ball. Players get the most touches when they do drills with just one partner.

The same drill is often run in four stages:

Practice makes the player.

Stationary drills (stage one): Players stand 10 yards (9.1 m) apart and throw to each other and catch while standing still. Remember to switch hands at some point.

Motion drills (stage two): Players perform the same skill while moving down the field together. Be sure to move both left and right.

Combination drills (stage three): Players perform more than one skill, such as a ground ball pick-up and a pass.

Defender drills (stage four): Skills are performed on the move with the introduction of a defender or defenders.

After the basic skills are mastered, players may move on to more complicated drills, such as "Simon Says," where a coach calls out the moves on the fly. Next, small scrimmages and short games may be introduced at practice. To get started, here are some basic sample drills.

WARM-UP SHUTTLE (BOYS AND GIRLS)

Players use this drill, also called a "train," to warm up at the start of practice and before a game. It gets their feet moving, gets them comfortable with their sticks, and allows them to practice accurate throwing and catching.

How to Throw

1. Begin with your top hand above and behind the shoulder. Think of the position your arm and hands would be in to throw a baseball or football.

2. Point the stick, and step toward the target onto the foot opposite the throwing hand.

Preparing to step toward the target for the throw.

3. Use the bottom arm to pull the butt of the stick toward the body. Think of an arc.

4. Use your top hand to make a wrist-snapping (as opposed to pushing) motion.

5. Be sure to follow through all the way. Don't stop short, or the ball won't go very far.

Learning to catch is key.

How to Catch

1. Place your top hand at the throat and your bottom hand at the bottom of the stick. Think of making your stick more like a baseball glove.

2. Put your stick in front of your face, in a protected and ready position.

3. Keep your eyes on the ball.

4. When you spot the ball, begin to move the head of the stick back and in the direction the pass is traveling.

5. Bend your elbows as you catch.

6. Cushion the ball in the pocket.

Catching the ball can be challenging. The ball has to land in your stick, and you must learn to cradle immediately to gain control of the ball and prevent another player from checking you.

The Drill: Part One   Three or four players line up single file, with another line of three or four players facing them 10 to 15 yards (9.1–13.7 m) away. The first player in line 1 has the ball and passes to the first player in line 2. Players run to the end of the opposite line after they complete their pass.

Players catch right, throw left. Then switch. Catch left, throw right.

As players progress, introduce specific catches, such as catching on the off-stick side or catching over the shoulder.

The Drill: Part Two   Do the same drill but instead of passing, players in line 1 throw a ground ball in front of the player in line 2 (called "ground balls to"), who then scoops it up and passes it back to the next player in line 1.

**Remember:
Work both sides.**

WARM-UP SHUTTLE TIPS

■ Coaches should only group three or four players to a line. They need to warm up, not stand around!

■ Add in additional skills or vary the shuttles. Also, as players improve, coaches should add in defenders so players learn to throw and catch under pressure.

CRADLING (BOYS AND GIRLS)

Cradling is a very important part of lacrosse and is the first skill most coaches teach. Players need to learn cradling, which is basically keeping the ball in the pocket by moving the stick in a semi-circular motion, before they can pass and shoot. Cradling is especially important in the girls' game since women's sticks don't have very deep pockets.

How to Cradle

1. Grasp the stick's shaft with the right hand by the throat of the stick, where the head meets the shaft. Try to hold your stick with your fingertips, not in your palm, for more flexibility.

2. Line up the "V" of the right hand, the space between the index finger and the thumb, with the center of the pocket.

3. Keep the stick tight by your body and up by your shoulder. When it's in your right hand, it should stay next to your right shoulder.

4. The left hand is at the end of the stick, positioned at waist height.

5. Move the stick in a semi-circular path between the middle of the body and the outside of the shoulder.

6. Switch sides.

Try a solid but flexible grasp.

The Drill Players line up in rows, three or four to a row. The first player in every line jogs down the field cradling his stick. The goal is not to drop the ball. Vary the drill by adding a defender to shadow the players' movements, or have a coach shout out different positions "high right . . . low right" while the players run.

As players progress, more advanced cradling techniques, such as a one-handed cradle, may be introduced.

CRADLING TIPS

- During drills *with* a defender, try to keep eye contact with your defender. If his eyes are locked with yours, he can't look at your stick. Player should use his body to defend his stick.
- During drills *without* a defender, your focus should be on the field—not the ground ahead of you or your coach. Don't look at your stick!

SCOOPING (BOYS AND GIRLS)

In youth lacrosse, the ball spends a lot of time rolling on the ground since players are still learning to catch the ball. But ground balls show up at all levels of lacrosse, so scooping or pick-ups are important to learn and master.

The Drill Players line up single file. The coach rolls the ball to each player, one at a time. The players run toward the ball, pick it up, pass it back to the coach, and then run to the end of the line and repeat.

Vary the drill as players improve by adding pressure. Form two lines, and have the first two players in each line compete for the ground ball.

Here's the scoop.

SCOOPING TIPS

- The top hand should be at the throat of the stick.
- Hands should be parallel to the ground.
- Players should step as close to the ball as possible.
- Accelerate when the ball enters your stick.
- Try to end up in a position prepared to make the next play.

STICK CHECKING (GIRLS)

Although youth players do not stick check—and no female players are allowed to body check—once players advance into high school and master the basic skills, they need to learn stick checking, which is the repeated motion a defender uses in the attempt to dislodge the ball from an opponent's stick.

How to Stick Check

1. Make sure the body is positioned correctly—feet facing forward, knees slightly bent, hip-to-hip with your attacker.
2. Make contact when the opponent's stick is vulnerable during the cradling motion.

3. Stay balanced in order to attempt multiple stick checks. Make repeated taps on the opponent's stick.

4. Keep the feet moving, and watch for a ground ball.

Pair up and check.

The Drill Players pair up and practice checking. One player remains in a stationary position, keeping one foot still and pivoting on the other as her defender moves around her attempting to check. Next, players move down the field in pairs, stick checking as they go.

STICK CHECKING TIP: Go for the corner of the opponent's stick head. Try to make the stick spin a little bit.

STICK CHECKING (BOYS)

When it comes to checking, boys have a lot more leeway than girls. All players except for Lightning and Bantam divisions are allowed to body check. Still, players cannot rely on body checking alone—it's all about stick skills. The most widely used stick check is the poke check, also called the "can opener."

How to Poke Check

1. Assume the ready stance, with the feet parallel.

2. Use the back hand to push the stick through the thumb and forefinger of the top hand.

3. Aim to position your body one stick's length away from the ball carrier

4. When the ball carrier has two hands on his stick, aim your poke at his bottom hand. If he has one hand on his stick, aim at the head of his stick.

The poke check.

The Drill Players line up about 10 yards (9.1 m) apart one-on-one. The offensive player has the ball and starts moving toward the goal. The defensive player attempts to force a turnover by poke checking. The drill can be performed with or without a goalie.

As players progress, have them add a lift at the end of the check to try to dislodge the ball, using the stick like a can opener.

POKE CHECK TIPS

■ When initiating a poke check, mimic the movement of shooting with a pool cue. Think of sliding the stick through the top hand.

■ All stick checks should be short, forceful, and controlled.

4-V-3 (BOYS AND GIRLS)

Defenders always try to guard or "mark" their assigned players to keep them from getting close to the goal and scoring. But sometimes, a player gets beat when an attacker makes a fast break, or in the boys' game, a player might be out serving a penalty, and his team finds themselves a "man down."

So players need to practice shifting their position, which is known as the defensive slide.

The Drill Four offensive players run down the field toward the goal as the coach tosses the ball to one of the players. The defensive player (one of three) closest to the player with the ball leaves her coverage, marks her, and does her best to slow her down. The rest of the defense shifts into place, anticipating where the ball will go next. The goalie is part of this too. She should leave the crease to intercept a pass if she has the opportunity rather than waiting for a shot on goal.

First, get the fundamentals. Then move on to drills that use multiple skills and mimic game situations.

Players mark their girl.

Prepare to slide.

4-V-3 TIP: Talk to each other on the field. Defenders should shout out information to their teammates, such as "Ball!" (meaning he's got the ball carrier) or "I've got two!" (meaning she's covering two attackers).

DODGES (BOYS AND GIRLS)

Every player, whether playing "O" (offense) or "D" (defense), needs to learn to dodge. On offense, this means outmaneuvering the opposition by rolling away from a defender, faking your movements so he runs the wrong way, or changing the location of your stick. There are several variations on dodge drills, which are usually done one-on-one.

The Drill

Pull dodge (part one): The ball carrier uses a quick stick movement to pull the stick away from the defender and keep the ball out of his reach.

Fake dodge (part two): Ball carrier places her stick in her dominant hand, then pulls it across her body so the defender thinks she is moving in that direction. She then shifts direction, utilizing a quick stutter step.

Split dodge variation: Player can also dodge by switching the stick from one hand to the other. Exaggerating the movement makes this dodge truly effective. Sell the fake.

Roll dodge (part three): The ball carrier completely turns his body around the opposing player, protecting the

Dodge ball: players practice "keep away."

Pivot to beat your defender.

stick and ball by holding it close to his body as he spins.

Rocker (part four): Same as a roll dodge, but the ball carrier turns halfway around, courtesy of a pivot, and then returns to his original position. Excellent move for when a defender is directly on an attacker's body. The goal is to end up directly behind the defender, not at an angle.

Reverse out (part five): For this dodge, the ball carrier attempts to beat her defender by simply changing direction.

DODGING TIPS

- While practicing dodges, don't do them at full speed.
- Protect your stick! If you extend your crosse away from your body while trying to dodge, you could get checked and lose the ball.
- On "O," be a good actor. Look where you want your defender to go, not where you intend to go.
- On "D," watch the offensive player's belly button. Even if his eyes say he's going right, if his belly button is pointed left, that's where he's likely to go.
- When your dodge is complete, accelerate immediately and head downfield.

Sell the fake.

SHOOTING (BOYS AND GIRLS)

Cradling, passing, and catching are important. But if a player can't shoot, he can't score. And that's the name of the game.

How to Shoot Shooting is much like passing, although it's almost always quicker and harder. Also, in shooting, the shooter can, and often should, aim for the ground. Basically, the movement is a fluid push and a pull. Players extend their arms all the way as they step through, in the direction of the goal, pushing the head of the stick forward, then pull the shaft back to the body. With practice, shots can be extremely accurate and fast.

Diagonal Shooting Drill This drill may be done with or without the goalie, but it's best to get the goalie in the cage for some practice. Players get in two diagonal lines. A coach or another player passes the ball to the front player in one of the lines, who runs toward the goal to take a shot. Shooters then run clockwise around to the back of the opposite line and get ready to shoot again as the front player in the other line takes a pass and runs to take a shot.

Vary this drill by adding a fake: as the shooter runs towards the goal, she exaggerates a fake (a dodging move), then takes a shot. Or, the coach or another player may roll the ball to the front player so that he has to scoop it first, then run and take the shot.

Shoot. Then shoot some more.

SHOOTING TIP: Since the goalie is standing in the goal, it's tempting for players to look at him and shoot at him. But the goalkeeper should not be your target. Aim for areas to the side of the goalie.

GOALTENDING (BOYS AND GIRLS)

Goalies get plenty of on-the-job training during practice. Every time a player shoots on goal, the goalkeeper gets a chance to make a save. But a chunk of time during every practice should be devoted to goalies practicing specific moves. Many coaches have goalies meet with them individually, apart from regular team practices, to improve certain essential skills.

Coaches emphasize a good goalie stance.

While field players are running passing and catching drills, a coach will often work with a goalie in the cage, focusing on one particular technique.

The Drill Three or four offensive players line up in a semicircle about 15 yards (13.7 m) from the cage and shoot long, low shots on goal. Vary the drill by switching to mid-waist shots and bounce shots.

Goalies in box lacrosse keep the heads of their sticks on the floor, while field lacrosse players stand with the head of the stick upright.

GOALTENDING TIPS

- Positioning is important for goalies. It's crucial to take a good solid stance.

- Don't just strap on your pads and go. Goalies need to properly warm up before stepping into the cage.

- Try to shadow the attacker, shifting your body to stay in line with his movements. Mirror the ball carrier when he is in front of you.

THE DRAW (GIRLS)

Every women's game begins—and restarts after a goal is scored—when the two centers, one from each team, meet midfield for the draw (also called the "center draw"). A ball is placed between their two sticks, which are pressed together back-to-back. Once the umpire calls "draw," the two centers compete to control the ball—picture the tip-off in basketball, only with sticks.

Players meet for the all-important center draw.

Once the whistle blows, the first player to get the ball on the back side of her stick "wins" the draw. So, at the whistle, she should immediately roll her wrist, then go after the ball by either pushing or pulling. A 2007 rule change states that "On the draw, a player's top hand may not contact any part of the sidewall or pocket of her stick."

The Drill Practice the draw by having two centers line up at the centerline, each one facing the goal she intends to attack. Each player has her toe on the centerline and her right hand at the top of the stick. (She places her left hand on top if her back is to her attacking goal.) Players hold their sticks back-to-back at or above waist level and parallel to the centerline. The referee places the ball between the sticks, then sounds the whistle. Players lift their sticks up, then away from their counterpart, to propel the ball into the air. Centers either push the ball to a teammate or pull it to themselves.

Position side by side. Ready, ref!

DRAWING TIPS

- Send four or five players to do draw work while others are running other drills.

- Add a component to the contest or drill for immediately after the draw: it's not always about who wins the draw or what direction the ball goes but who gets control of the ball afterwards.

- Later, add the rest of the team into the drill to practice what you do with the ball after the draw. Practice scenarios where your center wins and doesn't win the draw.

- Players should use both their upper and lower body strength to lift the ball.

At first, stay low.

THE FACE-OFF (BOYS)

The boys' and men's game begins, and restarts after goals scored, with a face-off at the center of the field. The opposing face-off players, who always take the face-off right-handed, facing their offensive goal, assume the face-off position and wait for the umpire to place the ball on the ground between them.

Note that the two wing midfielders from both teams also stand ready. Both attackers and defenders must remain in their respective areas until a loose ball enters the box area or a ref signals that one team has possession. During a face-off, the goal is for a player to either pull the ball to himself or push it to a teammate.

Face-Off Position

- Low and crouched, with feet placed shoulder-width apart.

Push or pull?

- Right hand is at the top of the shaft, palm facing forward. Left hand is shoulder-width from the top hand. Both hands should rest on the ground, with the shaft parallel to the midfield line.
- Place the stick 1 inch (2.5 cm) from the ball. Mirror the back of the pocket with your opponent's.
- Place both hands and feet to the left of the stick's throat.

The Drill   Players, including face-off opponents, take their position. Coach places the ball on the ground at the centerline and blows the whistle. Players go for the ball, and stop play after a team gets possession. Then, they do it again.

Many lacrosse players practice the clamp or "clamp and step" technique during the face-off.

Clamp-and-Step

1. At the whistle, stay low while stepping to the head of the stick. Clamp down on the ball with the right hand, and use your right shoulder to block the opposing player while pulling back with the left hand.

2. Move your head and upper body on top of the ball, and pivot the hips into your opponent so your body is positioned between him and the ball.

3. Pick up the ball, step out, and pass.

Players often rake the ball after they clamp it, which means they pull it to themselves. Players should also learn to rake right off the whistle, without clamping it first.

Face-Off Tips

■ The ball usually comes loose during a face-off, so be prepared to go after the ball in a crowd.

■ Even if your opponent gets the ball initially, don't back off! Try to jar it loose.

■ Keep both hands on the stick.

A Word About Drills

The drills listed above are only a few of the many practice exercises players may run to learn skills needed to play the game. There are many other drills to learn, for clearing, cutting, and crease defense, for instance, and quite a few excellent sources for additional drill options, such as the book *Coaching Youth Lacrosse*, which includes extensive lists of drills, many with diagrams and fun names such as Woodpecker, Monkey in the Middle, Hot Rock, and Center Circle Bulls Eye. There are also many excellent instructional DVDs featuring numerous drills available through the US Lacrosse Web site. Also check out Laxdrills.com.

Aerobic: A stage of a workout when all of the body's need for oxygen is met by what is being inhaled and what is already stored in the body. This state can continue for a long time.

Anaerobic: A stage of a workout when the body's need for oxygen is not met by what is being inhaled or by what is already stored in the body. This state cannot continue for a long time due to the buildup of lactic acid in the body, which results in a painful condition.

"D":   Short for defense.

"O":   Short for offense.

Drills: Practice exercises designed to mimic and improve game skills. The more elements included, the more effective the drill.

Push and pull method: A technique for winning the ball on the face-off or the draw.

Stickies: Nickname for stick tricks, or fancy moves performed with the crosse.

Touch: When a player makes stick contact with the ball.

Wall Ball: Exercises performed alone or in a group where a player tosses the ball against a wall and catches it.

Variety is the key to fun practices.

6: GAME DAY

Pre-Game Rituals and Top-Notch Tactics

As the oldest North American sport, lacrosse claims many traditions. Modern lax fans have been busy establishing new traditions, including the ritual of turning the play-offs and championship game of the NCAA into an exciting annual event. Fans love to watch big games where the best college players strut their stuff. But even youth games hold a special appeal for spectators.

"There's lots of scoring, and you have kids running into each other and whacking each other with sticks," said UVA coach Dom Starsia. "Lacrosse is not a hard sport for American spectators to enjoy!"

PRE-GAME

Before the players, coaches, refs, and fans come together for a game, every team prepares in its own way.

RITUALS

Like the baseball player who refuses to change his lucky socks, lacrosse players and coaches have their own superstitions and rituals. Navy coach Richie Meade has a ritual that actually involves good hygiene. Ever since his playing days, he's taken a pre-game shower in the locker room to guarantee that all the dirt he found on himself later came from playing the game.

Johns Hopkins coach Dave Pietramala, who arrives five hours before every game, has a slightly more intricate routine. First, he places the game plan and defensive keys up on the board. Then, he gets dressed and takes two laps around the Athletic Center before heading to his office. When the team leaves the locker room for official warm-ups, he and his assistant coach are

Even when your team is not playing at home, take the "Home Team Advantage" with you. Cheer each other on—loudly. The encouragement can mimic the support your team feels at home.

always the last two to go out. In previous years he would also get a package of peanut butter cups and place them on another coach's desk facing exactly the same way (he has since abandoned this tradition).

Towson head coach Tony Seaman has a purely practical pre-game ritual: He picks up stray balls around the field that were left behind after warm-ups.

Game Day Prep

Most lacrosse teams have a systematic way of preparing for a game. Especially at the college level, this process begins well ahead of actual game day. College teams often get detailed scouting reports about their opponents and study their offensive and defensive plays. Teams watch films and make notes about where a goalie makes most of her saves and whether certain players are right- or left-handed.

By game day, players are ready.

**Game day prep starts
with a warmup.**

GAME WEEK PREP

The strength and conditioning coach at Johns Hopkins and Calvert Hall recommends the following training tips for lax players the week before a game:

- Skills are key.

- It's all about intensity. Go all out, or don't go out at all.

- Quality not quantity.

- Technique is imperative.

- Rest, recover, and replenish.

Your focus before a game should be on your game. Spend most of your time during the pre-game week honing your lacrosse skills, but also make sure to include one or two lifting workouts and one or two conditioning workouts. During these workouts, your intensity should be high while the volume should remain low. Concentrate on your technique both in the weight room and on the field. Finally, make sure you give your body time to heal by eating well and getting plenty of rest.

Then, the team takes that information and incorporates it into practices during the week before a game. So, deep into the season, it's essential that the team be well versed in fundamentals and in excellent physical condition, so they can concentrate on the game at hand.

Once game day arrives, every team has its own style. Many players pump themselves up with loud music in the locker room. The coach will often go over game plans one more time and may also give an inspirational speech. Then, teams usually begin with an unstructured "throw around," where they hit the field and casually talk to each other as they pass back and forth, with no coaches on the field.

After their regular warm-up—jogging, stretching, drills—they'll be at game speed and ready to go.

PRE-GAME TIP: Even when a game starts early on a Saturday morning, players should make sure they eat something for breakfast. Try to at least have a granola bar or banana an hour or two before the game.

FIELD TACTICS

Game day has arrived, and your team is ready to go. You have scouted your opponent, or at least know their reputation, and you have a game plan. Every plan will be a little different, depending on the opponent's style.

But coaches and players shouldn't get too hung up on reacting to anticipated scenarios, although it's a great idea to practice as many scenarios as you can throughout the season. Every team should concentrate on playing to its own strengths.

Here are some game day strategies that always seem to translate into success on the field.

OFFENSIVE OVERVIEW

Every offensive player should study the following ten tips, as they apply to almost every game situation.

1. Keep moving all the time. Especially when you have the ball.

2. Vary your speed; don't run at the same pace all the time.

3. Learn as many types of dodges as you can—three at the very least—and be ready to use them!

4. Move to meet your teammates' passes, while circling away from your defender.

5. If a teammate is covered and can't get away, the nearest player should move in to assist him.

6. When the defense is clustered around the goal, don't try to force your way in by carrying the ball or by passing. Draw them out first.

7. Spread out. Don't allow one defender to cover you and another player at the same time.

8. If you don't have a clear shot or see an open teammate, hold on to the ball.

9. After scooping a loose ball, face the crease immediately. If no teammate is there to catch a pass, take the ball in yourself.

10. Only cut if the ball carrier is watching or in a position to pass.

Perhaps the number one thing offensive players should remember is that teamwork is the key to winning games. In lacrosse, teamwork is synonymous with passing.

The goal? Control the draw.

LUCK OF THE DRAW

In women's lacrosse, controlling the draw is one of the most strategic things a team can do. The player who can draw the ball, keep it, and run with it down the field is on her way to scoring. A very aggressive and tall center player who learns to push the ball straight up just may win the draw every time.

That said, other players can be just as important to the draw as the center. A really aggressive team can crash in and get the ball even if the center loses the draw.

Whenever possible, play it forward.

PASSING

Without question, passing is the fastest way to move the ball down the field.

Think about it: A player can whip a ball dozens of feet at a time, much farther than if she runs with it herself. The ball carrier has three pass options at her disposal: forward, lateral, or backward.

A forward pass is the most optimal since it progresses the ball toward the goal and a possible score.

A lateral pass is often used to get the ball to an area of the field that is less heavily defended.

A backward pass is executed when a team needs time to regroup.

MORE PASSING TIPS

- Passes should be made overhanded or underhanded, not side-armed.
- Passes should be short, crisp, and aimed to the outside of the defender.
- Never pass just to get rid of the ball, especially to a player who is being closely covered.
- Be sure to fake passes to throw off your defender.
- Keep the game moving at all times. Don't dodge if there is an open player. Pass!

You have to
shoot to score.

SHOOTING

Passing is essential. But shooting is what counts. Literally. Remember,
most shots are made on the run and not from a stationary position.
Here are some tips to increase your net gain.

- Shoot hard.
- Shoot often.

- Shoot deliberately and aim for a far corner of the cage. For very close shots, aim for the top corner of the cage.

- After taking a shot, move in and be ready to react. You may have a chance to take another shot if you miss and get the ball back.

- Before taking a really long shot, make sure a teammate is in position near the goal.

"The most dangerous place on a lacrosse field is "the island"—5 feet out and 5 feet up. This is the promised land for every attackman." —CMD COACH JEFF BEEKER

DEFENSE

Every player gets a chance to play defense at some point. When the other team has the ball, everybody on the opposing team wants it back. Here are ten things every defensive player should remember when the clock is running.

1. Always scoop a loose ground ball. Never draw it.

2. Move out to cover your player as the ball is moving toward him. Don't wait until he catches it to go after him.

3. Don't step into your player when playing D.

4. When your player doesn't have the ball, play slightly to the ball side of her. With this move you can gain a step if she cuts in the direction of the ball or will be in a good position to intercept.

Always scoop, never draw.

Stick up!

5. Don't carry your stick at your side. Keep it up!
6. Don't turn your back on the ball.
7. Make stick checks short, hard, and deliberate.
8. If your player dodges you, stay after him.
9. Never pass a ball directly in front of your team's goal.
10. Talk to each other.

Lacrosse is not a silent movie. When players are talking and fans are yelling, it's more like a blockbuster with *surround sound*.

D-TALK

Talk is all-important in lacrosse, especially on D. Players need to keep their teammates in the loop by communicating what's going on during the game. Players also need to let their teammates know when they need assistance—it's *okay* to holler for help. Here are some of the things defensive players might say, or more likely, yell to each other on the field.

- "Switch!" tells players to shift their coverage.
- "I've got the ball!" tells teammates a player is shifting his coverage to go after the player with the ball.
- "I've got your help" or "I'm one" tells a player his teammate has moved in to back him up.
- "I'm two" tells a player his teammate is his second back-up.
- "Man cutting!" alerts teammates that a player's man is cutting and they should prepare for a possible switch.
- "Pick!" alerts teammates to a pick.
- "Ball!" tells teammates a player sees and is going after a loose ball.
- "Man!" says a player who is within 5 yards (4.6 m) of a loose ball is attempting to body check or shield his opponent so a teammate can move in and scoop the ball. (*boys only*)
- "Release!" tells teammates a player has retrieved a loose ball.
- "Help!" alerts teammates that a player is open.

Talk it up.

For goalkeepers, the pressure is on.

ON GOAL

No defenseman is more important than the goalie. When new rule changes are introduced every year, it seems the game gets a little more competitive and tougher for the goalkeeper. For instance, a new women's rule states that offensive players' sticks, but not their bodies, may now

Game day is like exam day. If you're not ready, there isn't much more you can do.

enter the crease. Since the crease size hasn't increased, this means goalies face even more challenges. So, it's more important than ever for goalkeepers to have a foolproof game day plan.

GAME TIPS

Goalie at the ready.

- Keep your stick face flat to the shooter.
- Remember to keep your hands and elbows in front of your chest for all saves.
- Always keep your body balanced, in your ready stance.
- If the ball carrier runs behind the goal, the goalie should be out in front with her stick up. When the attacking player comes around, the goalie shifts to the post.
- Move outside the goal-mouth area when throwing a pass.
- Try to pass toward the side, not the middle of the field.
- When clearing the ball, slide the top and bottom hands 6 to 12 inches (15–30 cm) down the shaft for more power.
- Before clearing the ball, look where the shot came from. It's likely the player who made the shot is now covered with defenders.
- When clearing, look to the midfielders, who are most likely breaking away upfield.

Game day is a lacrosse player's chance to put into practice everything he's learned. But more importantly, it's his chance to go out and have fun. That's what lacrosse is all about.

7: CALL ME COACH

How to Build a Team—From Scratch

Because lacrosse is a relatively new sport in many parts of the country, someone interested in becoming a coach may actually have to start up the team. If the sport isn't sanctioned by a school, you may be talking about building the team from the ground up. Many coaches are doing this, especially those who were once players and who come from areas where lacrosse is popular. These new coaches are ambassadors for the sport.

Some very successful coaches have never even played the game. UVA's coach, Dom Starsia, who did play the game, has said, "You can develop a rudimentary sense of what's happening on the field fairly quickly if you grew up playing basketball or other team games. If you're honest and enthusiastic, you can impart that to your players and get good results. Kids are going to have fun, and that's a large part of it."

STARTING UP

So, if there's not an established team in your town looking for a coach, what's the best way to start from scratch?

GROUNDWORK

Step One: Recruit another coach, some assistants, and a few interested volunteers to help. Nobody can start and coach a team on her own.

Step Two: Find interested players. You need a team in order to coach it. Ask around and talk to kids. Consider recruiting players who have the season off from other sports.

Step Three: Research playing facilities: when they are available and what they will cost. Also research transportation options, such as buses or volunteers' vehicles. If players are going to have to pay to play, they will need to know this.

Step Four: Recruit a sponsor to pay for uniforms and equipment, or solicit donations from dedicated volunteers. Also, be sure to contact US Lacrosse to apply for an equipment grant awarded to teams in their first year of operation.

Step Five: Sign up for a US Lacrosse coach's clinic and an online coach's course. Contact other coaches in your area to get advice, and then immerse yourself in the rules for the age and level of play you will be coaching.

Step Six: Familiarize yourself with the concepts endorsed by the

Coaching starts with the basics.

Positive Coaching Alliance (PCA). Be sure to read *Positive Coaching* and *The Double Goal Coach* by Jim Thompson—take plenty of notes!

According to PCA founder and author Jim Thompson, the most important thing a new coach should remember is that every athlete has an "emotional tank" that needs to be filled for him to compete at his

> ## "What do I love most about coaching? The belly laughs." —MIDDLEBURY COACH MISSY FOOTE

best. "Coaches need to learn how to fill emotional tanks rather than drain them," Thompson has said. "A player whose coach fills his emotional tank will take criticism more to heart and will give their best for the coach and the team."

The key is to focus more often on what the player is doing right than on what he is doing wrong. Thompson even assigns a number: There should be five positives for every criticism. Remember, 5:1.

What Makes a Good Coach?

A lacrosse coach is a motivator, cheerleader, tactician, diplomat, role model, friend, teacher, and fellow fan of the game. Anyone who dedicates himself to this task needs to be committed to kids and truly have a love of the game.

According to Jim Thompson, there are three key ingredients to succeeding as a coach of young players.

1. Be a "Double Goal" coach. "Teachable moments present themselves constantly in youth sports, but they are lost if a coach is saddled with a win-at-all-cost mentality. Youth coaches who are not focused on both winning and using sports to teach life lessons should not be coaching kids."

Inspire kids to love the sport.

2. Increase players' love of the sport. "A great coach will inspire athletes to love the sport, to want to improve, and to want to come to practice."

3. Be an open communicator. "Include players in a conversation about the life of the team. Conversations are more effective than lectures. Ask for suggestions regarding the team's goals, strategies, and tactics, and include players in team decisions."

"Players have to understand that they are never going to be the most important thing, but that the team will always be the most important thing."—NAVY COACH RICHIE MEADE

You're in Charge. Now What?

Whether you're just starting out as a coach or you are an experienced coach beginning a new season with a new set of players, the most important thing to keep in mind is making sure your charges know the basics.

Build on Basics

According to Jeff Tambroni, men's head coach at Cornell University, "Like in any sport, the key to succeeding lies in the fundamental skills that are the foundation of every player's game."

University of Virginia men's head coach Dom Starsia agrees: "Young players should treat the game honestly from the beginning. That means learning the fundamental skills first before jumping ahead to some of the advanced moves they see on TV."

McDaniel College women's coach Meagan Voight says when kids hit the field in high school or college, it's easy to spot the players who have already mastered the basics at lower levels of play. "You can tell the ones who practiced a lot of throwing, catching, and cradling as opposed to just running," she said. "If kids didn't learn the fundamentals, then they'll be behind the other players."

So, first things first. Every coach needs to make sure his players know the basic moves of lacrosse, including cradling, passing, catching, scooping (ground balls), shooting, and dodging. These moves may be demonstrated by the coach or by more advanced players and then practiced during drills.

The best coaches fill their players' emotional tanks.

Start with simple drills, such as cradling, passing, and catching, and then move on to drills that incorporate several skills and feel more game-like. Make it fun by keeping score and awarding points for successfully completing skills. A little competition takes the drudgery out of drills.

TIP FOR THE COACH: New coaches can't learn all they need to know from a book. When it comes to coaching lacrosse, showing is often better than telling. Watch live practices run by more experienced coaches, and stock up on how-to DVDs you can reference often.

BE DELIBERATE

According to coach Missy Foote, "The same thing that makes a successful player makes a successful coach. That is, the ability to practice deliberately. As a coach, you need to recognize what you want to accomplish that day. Not your ultimate goal, such as winning a national championship or going undefeated, but determining what your team needs to do to get better and figuring out ways to make that happen."

Practice Makes Perfect

A player needs to improve the accuracy of his passes. Have him play Wall Ball with a specific goal of trying to hit the same spot ten times with his left hand, then his right hand.

Too many ground balls are hitting the field. This happens frequently with beginners. Have players line up for a basic passing and catching drill, emphasizing the basics of catching.

The goalie struggled during the last game. Instead of working on multiple skills, pick one technique to focus on during the next practice session. At the following practice, isolate another technique.

Fundamentals turn into serious fun.

TIP FOR THE COACH:

Take notes during a game regarding what needs to be addressed during the next practice. And do it!

PRACTICE PLAN

In the early 1990s, researchers at Michigan State University's Youth Sports Institute polled a group of young players who had dropped out of sports and asked them what would make them want to play again. The number one response? "If practices were more fun."

Young kids want to be active, so the better organized a coach is with his practice plan, the more fun players will have at practice. Jim Thompson recommends that every practice consist of the following:

- An opening ritual to signify the transition to being with the team.
- Team conversations. The coach engages the players in team business as opposed to standing up to lecture.
- Instruction in new skills and tactics.
- Conditioning.
- Scrimmaging.
- Drills and activities that remind players what fun it is to play lacrosse.
- Discussion of a life lesson. Relate what was learned in practice to other parts of players' lives.
- A closing ritual that sends them off with a positive feeling.

The best practices have a purpose.

TIPS FOR THE COACH

- Drills are an important part of lacrosse practice, and the best way to make them fun is by designing them to be multifaceted. Don't just make players run. Have them run while cradling the ball so they are conditioning and practicing a skill at the same time.

- Before a drill, pair up players with a buddy. During the drill each player has two responsibilities: perform the skills as best they can and fill the emotional tank of their buddy. Pump them up! Cheer them on! And talk about it afterwards.

- Don't be afraid to adjust the plan. If players have mastered a drill, move on!

- Most coaches don't just plan one practice at a time but rather they map out a full-season plan before the season begins. The book *Coaching Youth Lacrosse* has an excellent sample season plan for both boys and girls, with sample drills for every practice.

MOTIVATION

Every aspiring coach wants to know, how do I motivate my players? According to UVA's coach Dom Starsia, it's all about getting to know your players. "It's all an exercise in relationships," he said. "Coaches are motivating all the time. It never stops."

Middlebury coach Missy Foote agrees and takes another step. "It's my job as coach to motivate players by setting goals that are not unrealistic," she said. "Then, when a player needs to learn a skill, we put her in 'the hot seat.' We give her something to learn and make it really hard but still doable and game-like so she can get it. A coach should put players in uncomfortable situations until they become comfortable."

Not surprisingly, the PCA's Jim Thompson has a positive take on the concept of motivation. In his book *Positive Coaching*, Thompson describes an effective motivational technique called "positive charting." Basically, this involves keeping notes on each player's improvements and later sharing them with the entire team. Key aspects include:

1. Each player should have the same number of things noted and shared for each game, stars and weaker players alike.

2. Recognize kids for things they have done on their own as well as on what you are teaching.

3. Include character items when appropriate. (Example: Didn't lose temper.)

4. Give recognition for effort, not just for results.

5. Do note negative things during the game but don't share them with the kids at this time.

6. Ask kids to help you observe good things that other kids are doing.

7. After the last practice before a game, get together with your coaches and note what things you want to watch for with each kid during the next game.

Many coaches teach lacrosse skills by using the IDEA approach: Introduce, Demonstrate, Explain the skill, and Attend to players as they practice.

CALLING ON THE GIPPER

Every coach secretly pictures herself giving a famous Knute Rockne speech that will someday be immortalized on film. Or does she? Every coach has to find her own personal style when it comes to talking to

Show 'em what you know.

the team before or after a game. According to McDaniel College coach Meagan Voight, some of the best speeches she heard from coaches were extremely short: "You guys are ready. Let's go." Sometimes, less is more.

The same holds true for coaching from the sidelines during a game. Players appreciate specific instructions, "Get your man!" "Ball!" and plenty of positive reinforcement, "Good shot, Mary!" but players may begin to tune out a coach who hollers all the time.

WHO GOES WHERE?

One of a coach's most crucial roles is assigning players to positions. Most lacrosse players play several different positions in their career; many even switch positions several times within the same season.

According to coach Missy Foote: "At first glance, you're going to want to put your speedy players in the midfield, kids with a nose for the goal close to the goal on offense, and your grittier players on defense, but it isn't always like that. We move players around all the time."

Every coach has her own take on this task. For example, in the women's game, one coach may feel that it is essential to have her strongest player at center. Another may feel that any player can take the draw since she has placed her strongest players immediately outside the circle, feeling confident they can get possession of the ball regardless of what the center does during the draw.

It's a coach's job to convince his players to keep an open mind about swapping positions. After all, lax is the quintessential team sport, and no matter what position a player plays, he'll be relying on his teammates.

**Motivation:
A coach's number-
one job.**

Know the Scoop

Keeping track of the rules can be cumbersome for a coach. Within your own league, though, it fast becomes second nature. When traveling to an out-of-town tournament or playing against a team from another league, coaches will want to be sure to be up to snuff on the applicable rules.

- Know which set of rules the tournament will follow.
- Check them out ahead of time.
- Inquire about rule differences from other coaches or officials.
- Let your team know of any rules different from what they're used to well before game day.

SAFETY FIRST

As with coaches in any sport, a lax coach's most important priority should be the safety of his players. Every coach needs to make sure his players wear proper, well-fitting protective equipment. This should be covered the first day of practice. Encourage players to go beyond the minimum required padding and gear as long as they are comfortable wearing it. When it comes to protection, especially for goalies, *more is better*.

And, since a player can get hurt during practice just as easily as he can during a game, the coach needs to enforce safety rules on practice days the same way a referee would on game day.

Lacrosse, especially the men's game, has a reputation as a rough and tumble sport. Although the US Lacrosse Sports Science and Safety Committee has published statements backed up by numerous studies that lacrosse is relatively safe compared to other commonly played

THE FINE LINE

Many of the most legendary stories in sports have been told about players playing hurt or playing through pain. As inspiring as these stories can be, lacrosse coaches, especially those in charge of beginners, need to help their players decide when it's time to keep playing and when it's time to stop. Matthew Bussman, associate athletic trainer at Johns Hopkins University, says this is especially important when dealing with chronic injuries, which tend to resurface and last a long time.

"A red flag should go up if you start noticing a difference in your performance because of an injury," Bussman said. "If you think you could have beaten that girl or you could have gotten to that ball if your leg didn't hurt, then it's time to sit out." Bussman reminds his players to be smart athletes. "If they know they can take two days off now and be 100 percent by the weekend, then that's the smart thing to do. That will help the team the most."

Athletes never enjoy just sitting around. So, Bussman often involves his injured players in practice by having them do an alternative activity. For example, someone with an injured ankle may not be able to run but he could still do some partner passing. Or, while the rest of the team runs or does cutting drills, he can ride a stationary bike on the sidelines.

team sports, lacrosse involves intentional and unintentional contact, and a coach needs to be ready to address the inevitable injury.

Even though boys wear helmets, since players wield sticks, concussions are always a concern, especially in the girls' game. Coaches should learn about treatment for such an injury. US Lacrosse sells a tool kit for coaches entitled, "Heads Up: Concussion in High School Sports," produced by the Centers for Disease Control and Prevention (CDC). This is a must-have for lax coaches.

Coaches should also complete first aid and CPR training provided by a nationally recognized organization such as the American Red Cross or the National Safety Council. And every coach must always have a list of emergency numbers and a quality first aid kit on hand.

The first aid kit should include the following items:

- Cell phone
- Plastic bags (for ice)
- Mirror
- Flashlight
- Disposable plastic gloves
- Scissors
- Triangular bandages
- Roll gauze
- Adhesive tape
- Square gauze pads
- Cotton balls

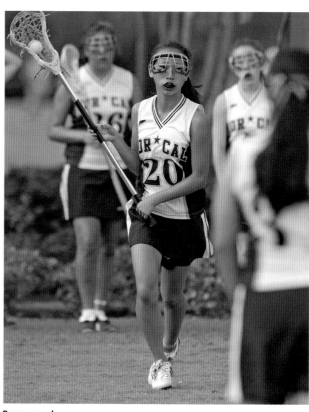

Pump up players with two- or three-part drills.

- Band-Aids (all sizes)
- Saline solution
- Tongue depressors
- Peroxide
- Antibacterial soap
- Hydrocortisone cream
- Insect sting kit
- Safety pins
- Thermometer

Just as important as a well-stocked first aid kit is a well-thought-out emergency plan. Coaches may ask a volunteer committee of parents to help organize the team's emergency plan, which should include creating an emergency response card that contains phone numbers and medical information on each athlete, and detailing how the team will deal with minor and major injuries.

PRICE

According to the American Sport Education Program, coaches should use the PRICE method when faced with an injured player:

P – Protect the athlete and injured body part from further danger or trauma.

R – Rest the area to avoid further damage and foster healing.

I – Ice the area to reduce swelling and pain.

C – Compress the area by securing an ice bag in place with an elastic wrap.

E – Elevate the injury above heart level to keep the blood from pooling in the area.

Got game?

LEND A HAND

It takes a village to play lacrosse, especially in areas where the sport is still growing and not yet state-sanctioned. There are many roles for people to play when they share the common goal of supporting the team.

THE ROLE OF PARENTS

Often, parents play the role of coach even when they don't have the official title. Parents cheer on their child and encourage him after he has a bad practice or a not-so-good game. The role of lacrosse moms and dads can't be overemphasized. Parents are often volunteers who keep the team alive by heading up car pools, leading fund-raising drives, or helping to line the field. Most importantly, they also support the coach.

US Lacrosse's Parents' Guide, with plenty of input from the Positive Coaching Alliance, put together the following tips for parents of young players:

One: Be supportive of your child by giving encouragement and showing an interest in his or her team. Positive reinforcement encourages learning and fun. Research has shown that a ratio of five positive statements (compliments, positive recognition) for each negative statement (criticisms, corrections) is ideal for helping young athletes do their best. Try to maintain a 5:1 ratio in your comments to your child.

Two: Attend games whenever possible. If you cannot attend, ask about your child's experience, not whether the team won or lost. Some questions that

Aim for an open dialogue between players and coach.

you might ask before asking about the final score include: "Did you try as hard as you could? Did you have fun? Did you learn anything today that might make you a better player in the future?"

Three: Be a positive role model by displaying good sportsmanship at all times to coaches, officials, opponents and your child's teammates. "Honoring the Game" is an important part of what US Lacrosse represents. Help us by honoring the game in your behavior as a spectator.

Four: Let your child set his own goals and play the game for himself. Be your child's "home court advantage" by giving him or her your unconditional support regardless of how well he or she performs.

Five: Let the coach coach. Refrain from giving your child advice when he or she is playing. Use positive reinforcement with your child's coach. Let the coach know when he or she is doing a good job.

Six: Respect the decisions of the referee or umpire. This is an important part of honoring the game. Your child will pay more attention to how you act than to what you say.

Seven: Read the rulebook. A full understanding of the rules will help you enjoy the game and educate others.

Eight: Get to know who is in charge. Meet with the leadership of the pro-

gram, whether it's school sponsored or recreational, to discuss topics such as cost, practice and game scheduling, insurance coverage, emergency procedures, etc.

Nine: *Get involved! There are many opportunities for volunteering.*

Ten: *Sit back and enjoy the game. Remember, lacrosse is played for FUN.*

Not ready to take the plunge and become a coach? There are many other ways parents of young lacrosse players can get involved and support their child's team. According to US Lacrosse, volunteers are always needed to:

- Assist the coach
- Keep score
- Run the clock
- Line the fields
- Manage equipment
- Chaperone trips

CALLING ALL PLAYERS

The scholarship opportunities for college players are rising dramatically. Parents may want to know what one top college coach is looking for in a player:

Dave Pietramala, head coach at Johns Hopkins, says: "We are always searching for great student athletes that are big, strong, and have very good skills. However, there are intangibles that are very important to our staff. We want to attract great people, young men that will work hard in the classroom and on the field. We are always looking for leaders, guys that separate themselves from their peers. We are anxious to attract young men that understand the game and that have a passion for our sport. There is no overlooking the guy that does the little things like hustle to a huddle, congratulates the teammate that passed him the ball when he scored a goal or the player that arrives first to practice and is the last to leave. Those guys usually become the great ones."

Start 'em young.

- Organize a booster club and manage the club's activities
- Raise funds
- Organize advertising, marketing, and publicity for the team
- Organize coach and player clinics
- Hold cookouts and social events
- Organize carpooling to practices and games
- Assist in making schedules
- Assist during registration
- Photograph players and games
- Create a yearbook or program
- Take children to local and national lacrosse games and events

HEY COACH!

According to the PCA, here are a few things parents want from a coach:

- To be in the information loop
- To hear good things about their kids
- To see their kids play
- To be included and recognized (for example, by a coach learning their name)

Parents are also crucial to a team's success in that cooperative parents who support the coach and are respectful to the referees help the game grow. If referees and coaches aren't treated decently, they won't continue to volunteer their time. And both are desperately needed in youth lacrosse.

What coaches appreciate perhaps most of all from parents is the opportunity to "borrow" their children for one, two, or even four years.

When asked what they love about coaching, almost every coach cites the opportunity to watch a young player develop and evolve during the time she spends with her. "How many 53-year-olds have twenty-five 18-year-olds in her life?" said Coach Missy Foote. "There's always something funny or silly going on to laugh about. For me, the challenge is to bring a different group of kids together and get them to perform at the highest level. Better than they were before. That never gets old for me."

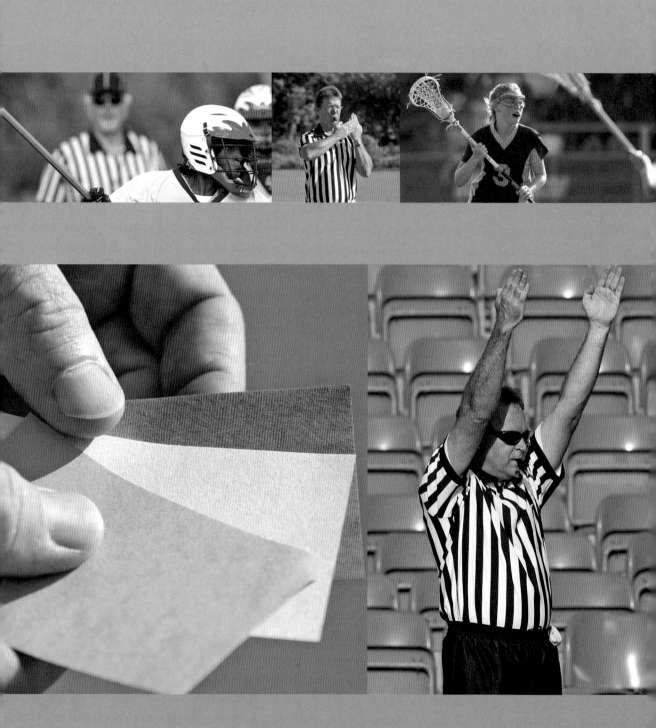

8: It's Official

The Judges and Jury of the Game

Officials are essential to lacrosse. Games can't happen without them. Graduating college players or ex-high school players make excellent candidates. So do coaches and parents who may have never played but have been involved with their children playing the sport. Coaches and parents have also found lax officials by recruiting refs from other sports, especially those which share some common ground with lacrosse, such as hockey, soccer, and basketball.

Many lacrosse games come and go without anyone ever noticing the umpires on the field. And that's a good thing. When officials are invisible, they probably called a good game.

LACROSSE UMPIRES AND REFEREES

There is no better way to give back to the sport you love and keep kids playing than by volunteering as a referee. Good refs are equal parts diplomat, psychologist, boss, teacher, athlete, team player, lacrosse enthusiast, and invisible man.

BECOMING A REFEREE

Due to the explosive growth of lacrosse, there is an enormous demand for qualified officials, especially at the youth level. Most referees begin their officiating career in youth leagues and later, if interested, work their way up to the high school or college level. Some officials remain youth officials indefinitely, which is good news for all those young athletes.

So, what's the first step?

First, a potential ref should have some knowledge of the game. Begin by reading, watching DVDs, and attending games to become familiar with lacrosse. Resources such as *Referee Magazine* include articles on a variety of issues, including how to deal with rising tempers.

In early Native American lacrosse games, medicine men were the officials. They blessed equipment, led pre-game ceremonies, and determined the rules. They also were in charge of keeping score, utilizing a sharp knife to notch each goal on a special stick.

Refs on the run.

Next, talk to lacrosse parents, coaches, or other refs to gather more information. US Lacrosse offers different levels of training through the Men's and Women's Division Official Councils (MDOC and WDOC). Contact US Lacrosse to be put in touch with local officials and find out about training dates in your area. Also note that basic training costs about $20.

EARNING YOUR STRIPES

US Lacrosse Level 1 training is meant for those with little or no experience officiating lacrosse, including youth and beginning officials of any level. The goal is to introduce new referees to the basic rules and mechanics needed to facilitate a safe and fair game.

Officials will learn to:

■ Properly prepare individually and with a partner(s) in advance of contests.

■ Maintain a safe level of play at each contest.

■ Communicate effectively with voice and hand signals [with partner(s), coaches, and the scorer's table].

■ Understand and correctly demonstrate basic field positioning.

■ Correctly identify if a team has possession of the ball in a penalty situation and how to apply the slow whistle technique.

■ Understand and recognize differences between personal and technical fouls.

■ Recognize and assess the most common safety fouls accurately and fairly.

US Lacrosse Level 2 training is meant for those with field experience and an understanding of basic rules and mechanics. The goal is to advance officials' knowledge and application of rules, mechanics, and game management.

Officials will learn to:

■ Maintain a safe environment at each contest (on and off the field).

■ Establish a confident, professional, and authoritative presence on the field.

■ Communicate effectively with a clear, commanding voice and demonstrative hand signals [with partner(s), players, coaches, and the scorer's table].

■ Understand and correctly demonstrate advanced field positioning.

■ Correctly identify which team has possession of the ball in a penalty situation and the sequence of fouls as they occur.

Refs dress the part.

■ Understand, recognize, and assess all fouls, including simultaneous fouls and fouls that create an advantage.

■ Recognize advantage/ disadvantage in loose ball situations and when and why the play-on technique is required.

■ Assess all fouls accurately and fairly.

Still want to earn your stripes? According to US Lacrosse, here's what you'll need to do:

1. Attend a US Lacrosse training course. You'll receive a Level 1–2 training manual, rule book, instruction from an approved trainer, and eventually, a rules test.

2. Establish, renew, or maintain current official category membership with US Lacrosse. This provides liability coverage and other important member benefits.

3. Finish your training. Upon completion, your trainer will send a training notification form to US Lacrosse. You'll be in the database and eligible to be put on a schedule.

4. Wear your patches. Two are awarded upon completion of training. Refs may purchase up to four more patches a year.

5. Stay current. Sign up for extra training events and check out tips online and in periodicals such as *Lacrosse Magazine* or *Inside Lacrosse*.

WHAT DOES A REF DO?

A referee has many different jobs. He's got to check equipment, approve the playing field, make the calls, and keep the game moving. But his key role and primary focus at all times should be on safety. Every duty he performs is to ensure the safety of the players, the spectators, and also himself and his fellow referees.

When he checks players' equipment before the game, he is making sure that one player doesn't have an unfair advantage over another player. But perhaps more importantly, he is ensuring that a stick or piece of protective equipment won't inflict harm on anyone who is on the field.

Refs keep the game moving.

When he spots a player pushing and calls a foul, he is removing an unfair advantage. But more importantly, he is preventing one player from possibly injuring someone else.

Pre-Game Duties

- Check players' equipment.
- Check the field markings and set-up.
- Make sure the host team has made the field safe (e.g., no glass or stones) and provided items such as a clock and timekeeper's horn.

When game time approaches, the referee gathers team captains together for a coin toss. The winning team chooses the end of the field it wants to defend first. Boys' teams change sides between periods; girls swap sides at the half.

The teams grab their sticks and take their positions while the ref, whistle in hand, readies the ball for the face-off or draw. Once the ball is dropped the players burst into action. For the rest of the game, it's the officials' job to keep the ball moving whenever possible. Even when a foul occurs, officials will often elect to hold the whistle when an advantage to the offender is not evident.

As always, the top priority is keeping the game safe. Everyone involved in lacrosse should respect the fact that officials have authority over the game and also have jurisdiction over the timekeeper, scorer, players, substitutes, coaches, and anyone else affiliated with either team, including spectators. Further, it is understood that umpires have the authority to penalize any unsafe play not specifically outlined in the rules.

Make It Official

It is recommended that at least two officials be on hand at every lacrosse game. Lower-level youth games may be played with just one official, but games at the high school level and up are often played with three officials on the field (an umpire, referee, and field judge, for example) and one bench official on the sidelines.

Also, the terms "umpire" and "referee" that refer to field officials are often used interchangeably.

Officials' gear includes the following:

Uniform

- Striped shirt or jacket
- Patches
- Hat (either wool blend or mesh)
- Comfortable black shoes or cleats
- Knee socks
- White pants or shorts (men)
- Black pants, shorts, or skirt (women)
- Belt

Equipment

- US Lacrosse membership card
- Rule book
- Whistle(s)
- Scorecard and pencil
- Coin (for the toss)
- Tape measure
- Timing device
- Yellow flag (penalty marker)
- Green, yellow, and red warning cards (women)
- Clock and horn (timekeeper)
- Gear bag

FOULS AND PENALTIES

In lacrosse, penalties are categorized by how serious they are. In boys' lacrosse, fouls are personal (serious) or technical (less serious). In girls' lacrosse, fouls are major (serious) or minor (less serious).

Depending on the league and level of play, lesser fouls usually elicit a warning from the ref or play may be stopped and the ball may be turned over to the other team. More serious fouls result in anything from a 3-minute suspension to expulsion from the game.

TIP OFF

Every referee is different, so to some degree, players may want to "play to the referee." Pay attention to what happens at the beginning of a game. You can usually tell in the first few minutes what will cause the officials in a particular game to blow the whistle.

GIRLS' FOULS

Every referee should be well versed in what constitutes a foul in lacrosse. Players should study their particular rule books, which are extremely specific, and work closely with their coach to learn how not to foul other players.

In general, girls' game fouls are:

Major:

Blocking: Occurs when contact is initiated by a defender who has moved into the path of an opponent with the ball without giving that player a chance to stop or change direction.

Charging: Occurs when a player charges, barges, shoulders or backs into an opponent, or pushes with the hand or body.

Dangerous Propelling: Occurs when a player propels the ball without control in the direction of another player.

Dangerous Shot: Occurs when a player shoots the ball dangerously and without control and is most often called when the ball forcefully contacts the goalkeeper's helmet or facemask.

Misconduct: Occurs when a player conducts herself in a rough, dangerous or unsportsmanlike manner, persistently causes infringement of the rules, or deliberately endangers the safety of opposing players.

Slashing: Occurs when a defender swings her crosse at an opponent's crosse or body with deliberate viciousness or recklessness, whether or not the opponent's crosse or body is struck.

WARNING CARDS

Umps play with a full deck.

In the women's game, green, yellow, and red warning cards are used to penalize poor conduct. Each color signifies a different penalty, and used in combination, cards have different meanings. For example, a green card indicates delay of game. The second delay of game would warrant a green and yellow card and a third delay of game would result in a green and red card, whereby a player must leave the game for 3 minutes.

By themselves, cards mean:

Red: Player is ejected from the game due to a flagrant foul.

Yellow: Player must leave the field for 3 minutes (substitute allowed).

Green: Warning, delay of game.

Note: A 2007 rule change further states:

If a team receives three cards (yellow or red) for offenses occurring on the field of play, on the fourth and every subsequent yellow or red card the carded player must leave the field and no substitute may take her place for 3 minutes of elapsed playing time.

Three Seconds: A defender may not stand within the eight-meter arc for more than three seconds unless she is closely marking an opponent within a stick's length.

Obstruction of Free Space: Occurs when a defender is not closely marking her opponent, within a stick's length of an opponent and is in the free space to goal of the attack player with the ball. The attack player must have the opportunity and be looking to shoot.

Minor:

Goal Circle Fouls: Occurs when any part of an offensive or defensive player's body or crosse, except that of the goalkeeper or deputy, enters the goal circle.

Warding Off: Occurs when a player guards a ground ball with her crosse or foot, removes one hand from the crosse and uses her free arm to ward off an opponent.

Empty Crosse Check: A player may not check or hold an opponent's crosse unless the ball is in contact with the opponent's crosse.

Body Ball: A ball that rebounds off of a field player's body to her or her team's distinct advantage.

For youth modifications, see US Lacrosse youth rules. One notable difference: in Level C, all free positions are indirect (the player with the ball may never shoot directly from the free position).

GIRLS' PENALTIES

Penalties are the result of a foul or infraction of the rules by a player. In other words, penalty equals punishment.

US Lacrosse women's rules state:

The penalty for fouls is a free position. For major fouls, the offending player is placed four meters behind the player taking the free position. For a minor foul, the offending player is placed four meters off, in the direction from which she approached her opponent before committing the foul, and play is resumed. When a minor foul is committed in the critical scoring area, the player with the ball has an indirect free position, in which case the player must pass first or be checked by an opponent.

Note:

A slow whistle occurs when the offense has entered the critical scoring area and is on a scoring play and the defense has committed a major foul. A flag is displayed in the air but no whistle is sounded so that the offense has an opportunity to score a goal. If the offense is capable of getting a shot off, the flag is withdrawn. A whistle is blown when a goal is scored or the scoring opportunity is over. An immediate whistle is blown when a major foul, obstruction of shooting space occurs, which jeopardizes the safety of the player.

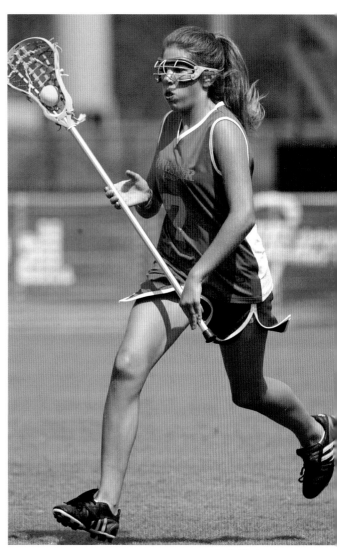

The ball's in play.

BOYS' FOULS

Rule books for each level of boys' and men's lacrosse list extremely detailed descriptions of what *not* to do while playing the game. Umpires and players should be well aware of these rules. In general boys are penalized for the following fouls:

One of an umpire's biggest challenges is learning how to be in position to make the call. If you're calling a game with two refs, your position will be different than if there are three of you.

Personal:

Cross Checking: Occurs when a player uses the handle of his crosse between his hands to make contact with an opponent.

Illegal Body Checking: Occurs when any of the following actions takes place:

A: body checking an opponent who is not in possession of the ball or within five yards of a loose ball;

B: avoidable body check of an opponent after he has passed or shot the ball;

C: body checking an opponent from the rear or at or below the waist.

D. body checking an opponent above the shoulders. A body check must be below the shoulders and above the waist, and both hands of the player applying the body check must remain in contact with his crosse.

Illegal Crosse: Occurs when a player uses a crosse that does not conform to required specifications. A crosse may be found illegal if the pocket is too deep or if any other part of the crosse was altered to gain an advantage.

Illegal Gloves: Occurs when a player uses gloves that do not conform to

Box Notes

required specifications. A glove will be found illegal if the fingers and palms are cut out of the gloves, or if the glove has been altered in a way that compromises its protective features.

Slashing: Occurs when a player's stick viciously contacts an opponent in any area other than the stick or gloved hand on the stick.

Tripping: Occurs when a player obstructs his opponent at or below the waist with the crosse, hands, arms, feet or legs.

Unsportsmanlike Conduct: Occurs when any player or coach commits an act which is considered unsportsmanlike by an official including taunting, arguing or obscene language or gestures.

Unnecessary Roughness: Occurs when a player strikes an opponent with his stick or body using excessive or violent force.

Technical:

Crease Violation: Occurs when an offensive player deliberately, through his own momentum, enters the opponent's goal-crease or a defensive player, including the goalkeeper, with the ball in his possession, enters from the surrounding playing field into his own goal-crease.

Holding: Illegally impedes the movement of an opponent with the ball.

Illegal Offensive Screening: Occurs when an offensive player, through moving contact of his body or equipment, blocks a defensive player from the man he is playing, or impedes his normal movements of playing defense.

Interference: Occurs when a player interferes in any manner with the free movement of an opponent, except when that opponent has possession of the

Box lacrosse, especially pro boxla, is a very different game than high school or youth field lacrosse with an entirely different set of fouls and penalties. This is the one version of the game where spectators will see fights (strictly forbidden at the youth level) and certain moves such as slashing, which is only penalized when it is "excessive."

Fans also enjoy an extremely fast-paced game, courtesy of the 30-second rule, which dictates that the offense must take a shot within 30 seconds or lose possession of the ball.

ball, the ball is in flight and within five yards of the player, or both players are within five yards of a loose ball.

Offsides: Occurs when a team does not have at least four players on its defensive side of the midfield line or at least three players on its offensive side of the midfield line.

Pushing: Occurs when a player thrusts or shoves a player from behind.

Stalling: Occurs when a team intentionally holds the ball, without conducting normal offensive play, with the intent of running time off the clock.

Warding Off: Occurs when a player in possession of the ball uses his free hand or arm to hold, push or control the direction of an opponent's stick check.

Withholding the Ball from Play: Occurs when a player clamps a loose ball against the ground more than momentarily or clamps the ball against his body to prevent it from being dislodged.

Youth rules list additional fouls, including:

Personal and Expulsion Fouls:

A. *Personal Foul/Slashing: (for Lightning and Bantam Divisions) Any poke check not making contact with the gloved hand while holding the stick or the stick itself will be considered a slash. Also, any one-handed check will be considered a slash for the Bantam Division.*

B. *Any player or coach who uses derogatory or obscene language on the field or bench, whether addressing a player, coach or referee may receive: first offense, a one-minute non-releasable penalty; a two-minute non-releasable penalty for the second offense; and expulsion from the game for the third offense.*

C. *Players illegally playing down to any division will be expelled for the season and the team will be eliminated from any playoffs and ineligible for any titles or awards.*

Also:

Body checking is permitted in Senior & Junior Divisions, however no take-out checks are permitted. Players may make contact in an upright position within five yards of the ball. No body checking of any kind is permitted in the Lightning & Bantam Division, which includes no man/ball, clear-the-body type pushing. If the ball is not moving, the referee will start play following the alternative possession rule.

Technical Fouls:

A. Offensive stalling shall be enforced, however this rule will be waived for Lightning and Bantam Divisions.

BACK-UP OFFICIALS

The lacrosse community is proud of its "Honor the Game" philosophy. One of the most positive offshoots of this mindset, and the partnership between US Lacrosse and the Positive Coaching Alliance, is the Sportsmanship Card program, whereby a sideline manager (a volunteer other than a referee or other official) is authorized to distribute a warning card to any coach, athlete, fan, or group of fans exhibiting bad behavior at youth games.

According to US Lacrosse, the sideline manager's role is:

To maintain a positive and sportsmanlike environment around the playing field, including both sidelines. The officials will handle on-field sportsmanship issues.

Behavior that does not "Honor the Game" includes:

- Entering the field of play, bench, or table area
- Throwing objects onto the field
- Continued berating of officials or others involved with the game
- Verbal threats of bodily harm, injury, or death
- The use of obscene or highly abusive language
- Fighting

The card is meant as a preventive tool to keep bad behavior from getting out of control. If the warning doesn't work, the officials will stop the game.

The Sportsmanship Card reads as follows:

Honor the Game.
Please rethink your actions. Your current behavior is contrary to the high level of sportsmanship expected of fans and participants at all events sponsored by US Lacrosse. This event may be terminated if your conduct does not improve.

B. Senior and Junior Division: the winning team is to keep the ball in the box during the last two minutes of the game. Lightning and Bantam Divisions are excused from this rule.

BOYS' PENALTIES

According to NFHS rules:

The penalty for a personal foul shall be suspension from the game of the offending player for one to three minutes, depending on the official's judgment of the severity and perceived intent of the personal foul. The ball shall be given to the team fouled.

The penalty for a technical foul shall be either a 30-second suspension of the offending player from the game (if the team fouled had possession of the ball at the time the foul was committed) or simply the awarding of the ball to the team fouled (if the team fouled did not have possession of the ball at the time the foul was committed).

Additional notes for youth players' penalties include:

Time-serving penalties are enforced and man-up situations are permitted in all divisions except the Bantam Division where there are no time serving penalties. Instead, the player must be substituted and the ball awarded to the other team at the point of the infraction.

IN HER SHOES

Missy Foote, a longtime women's lacrosse coach at Middlebury College in Vermont, says she never realized what a tough job referees have until she tried it herself while taking a break from coaching. "It was the hardest thing I've ever done," said Foote. "I promised at that point that I would never criticize another ref because I realized how hard it was."

Vigorous play.

Foote also said even when she disagrees with a referee's calls or an official's handling of certain game day situations, she tries never to let that affect her own decisions. "I really feel like referees don't control the outcome of the game," she said. "I love and respect our officials. It's their goal to be fair."

Officials would be happier people if every coach stepped into their shoes at least for a day. Even if coaches and players figuratively put themselves in a ref's position, it would go a long way.

Conversely, before he dons his stripes, every referee would be well advised to imagine the game from a player's point of view. "As a player, I like refs to let us play!" said former Johns Hopkins player Meagan Voight. "Good college refs will let the teams push a little bit and get a little rough. Obviously a ref needs to step in if things get out of control. But I think they should let it go as long as there's nothing serious going on. That's why the advantage call (where in women's lacrosse, the umpire will hold a flag in the air but not blow the whistle) is such a good idea. If I'm an attacker and the defensive player is pushing me, I'd rather beat them and score than have the referee blow the whistle."

"A ref's job is enforcing the rules, not interpreting them."—MISSY FOOTE, WOMEN'S HEAD COACH, MIDDLEBURY COLLEGE

THE CALLS

An official need to know the signals required to call the game. Consult a rule book for more extensive ref signals.

CALLS FOR GIRLS

Here are the basic calls for girls that umps, as well as fans and players, should know:

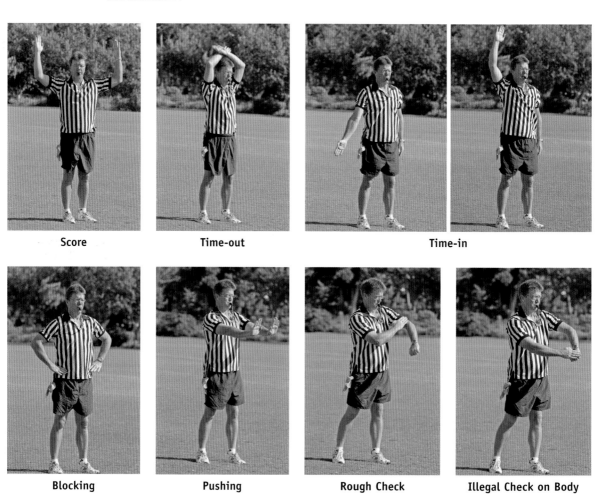

Score · Time-out · Time-in

Blocking · Pushing · Rough Check · Illegal Check on Body

Illegal Ball off Body

Obstruction of Free Space

Empty Crosse Check

Goal Circle Foul

Free Position—
Held Whistle

Re-draw

CALLS FOR BOYS

Here are the basic calls for boys that umps, as well as fans and players, should know:

Score   Play on   Tripping   Pushing

Holding   Illegal Body Check

Cross Checking

Offsides

Crease Violation

Interference

Slashing

Unnecessary Roughness

Unsportsmanlike Conduct

Warding Off

Stalling

Illegal Offensive Screening

A ref makes the call.

WOMEN

Arc: A pie-slice shaped area marked in front of each goal circle, at a distance of 26.3 feet (8 m), and bound by a straight line on the sides that is at a 45-degree angle to where the goal line extended meets the goal circle. Used to define 3-second violations and in the administration of major fouls. The 26.3-foot (8-m) arc is painted on the field and fits within the fan.

Direct free position: The result of a major foul in which the player awarded the ball may shoot immediately, run, or pass the ball to a teammate.

8-Meter Arc: A semi-circular area in front of the goal used for the administration of major fouls. A defender may not remain in this area for more than 3 seconds unless she is within a stick's length of her opponent.

Free position: An opportunity awarded to the offense when a major or minor foul is committed by the defense. All players must move 13.2 feet (4 m) away from the player with the ball. When the whistle sounds to resume play, the player may run, pass, or shoot the ball.

Indirect free position:	An opportunity awarded to the offense when a minor foul is committed by the defense inside the 39.4-foot (12-m) fan. When the whistle sounds to resume play, the player may run or pass, but may not shoot until a defender or one of her teammates has played the ball.
Penalty lane:	The path to the goal that is cleared when a free position is awarded to the attacking team.
Stand:	All players, except the goalkeeper in her goal circle, must remain stationary following the sound of any whistle.
Sphere:	An imaginary area, approximately 7 inches (18 cm), which surrounds a player's head. No stick checks toward the head are allowed to break the sphere.
12-Meter Fan:	A semicircle in front of the goal used for the administration of major and minor fouls.

MEN

Box (or penalty box):	An area between the two team's benches used to hold players who have been served with penalties and through which substitutions "on the fly" are permitted directly from the sideline onto the field.
Extra man offense (EMO):	A man advantage that results from a time-serving penalty by the other team.
Man down defense (MDD):	Refers to the defense when it is outnumbered as a result of one or more of its players serving time in the penalty box.
Take out checks:	Checks in which the player lowers his head or shoulder with the force and intent to take out (put on the ground) another player.
Turnover:	Losing possession of the ball without taking a shot, such as off a bad pass, when checked off the ball, or committing a violation.
Violation:	An action that causes the team to lose possession of the ball.

Longtime official and Hall of Fame inductee Jackie Hufnell told a reporter, "Every one of us (officials) strives for, 'They don't know we're there.'"

AFTERWORD

Lacrosse players and enthusiasts are fond of saying that if you put a stick in a young child's hands you've got a player for life. There's something about the stick and the movement of the game that hooks young athletes. Once they get out on the field and realize this is a game that involves the entire team most of the time—and that everyone plays and anyone can score—then you've really got 'em.

Lacrosse still has a long way to go in terms of becoming a mainstream sport. It's still a challenge to find lacrosse games on TV, and many players whose schools don't sanction the sport still have to form their own clubs and pay to play. Plus, it's difficult to expand lacrosse at the college level, especially at schools with large football programs.

But there are so many encouraging trends involving the game, chief among them the alignment of US Lacrosse with the Positive Coaching Alliance. By introducing and reinforcing the positive philosophies of the PCA at the earliest level, they actually become part of lacrosse.

Another encouraging trend is the emphasis on safety. US Lacrosse has a very active safety committee, and many teams and manufacturers commit a great deal of effort to research. Johns Hopkins lacrosse team trainers are working with STX to develop gloves that prevent thumb injuries, just to name one example. Every year, new standards are introduced and embraced by teams at all levels.

The most significant growth in lacrosse has come at the youth level. Today, there are dozens of camps operating around the country all summer long, giving new players a chance to learn the sport and more experienced players a chance to hone their skills. At the tournament level, the annual US Lacrosse Youth Festival, where more than one hundred teams from all over the country compete, is a shining example.

As lacrosse continues to grow, the goal is to keep the tight-knit spirit of the community intact. This can be accomplished when people who love the game continue to be involved as players, coaches, refs, and supportive parents.

One for all.

Appendixes

Strength and Speed Development for Lacrosse*

Proper strength development in sports is often misunderstood and neglected. For those few programs that include a strength and conditioning program for their athletes, the methods used are rarely optimal. One of the biggest problems that I see in many training regimens is the use of a bodybuilding style of weight lifting. This is an ineffective and often counterproductive method for a developing athlete. In order to build a strength-training program that will produce long-term results, it's important to first understand the role of strength in sports.

A quality strength-training program should have two main goals: the improvement of force production and injury prevention. Force production is the ability to display power and explosive strength in a given movement. Increasing an athlete's strength is one method of making him or her faster, as it will improve the ability to produce force into the ground while running. The role of strength training in injury prevention pretty much speaks for itself. By strengthening the muscles and connective tissue around the joints, athletes are much less susceptible to injury.

---

*By Brian Yeager (owner of Pro Strength Performance System, founder of Lax Speed, and strength and conditioning coach for the Philadelphia Barrage)

There are three types of strength that must all be addressed when designing a strength-training program for athletes of all ages. The methods used may vary depending on a player's age and physical readiness, but all are equally important. The three methods are outlined below:

Maximal effort (ME): This method refers to lifting weights that are maximal (90%+ of your max strength)

Dynamic effort (DE): This method utilizes sub-maximal loads moved as quickly as possible.

Repetition effort (RE): The repetition method uses sub-maximal weights lifted to failure or near failure.

SPEED DEVELOPMENT FOR LACROSSE

On the playing field, speed is king. While the more talented athlete will always dominate, an athlete with less talent can dramatically shorten the gap by following a speed development program. The ability to cover the field with blazing speed and change direction on a dime will go a long way in improving overall performance.

Athletes should address three main areas:

Starting speed: This refers to an athlete's ability to initiate action in the appropriate direction as quickly as possible.

Acceleration speed: This is the ability to transition from that initial, explosive movement to top running speed as efficiently as possible.

Change of direction: This refers to the ability to perform well-coordinated fluid changes of movement.

There are only three primary methods that may be used to increase running speed. While there are others, it is usually only necessary to focus on those mentioned below:

Stride frequency: The amount of strides taken in a given amount of time

Stride length: The distance covered by each stride

Running mechanics: The mechanics of running can be complicated and are best improved under the guidance of a qualified coach with a background in track and field.

The first two, stride frequency and length, are easily improved in the developing athlete through strength training. As mentioned earlier, weight training can increase force production. Driving into the ground with more force will immediately increase the speed of the movement and the distance covered with each stride. For most young athletes, this will be enough to improve their playing speed. Proper running mechanics are something that should be emphasized and worked on during every speed-training workout.

The following template is a sample strength and conditioning workout for a high school lacrosse player. It is important to note that the regimen provided assumes a certain level of physical readiness in the athlete. A properly designed program will follow a progressive approach based on the individual accomplishments of each athlete.

Monday: power clean (DE), back squat, (ME), Romanian deadlift (RE), bench press (ME), wide-grip pull-ups (RE), weighted crunches (RE).

Tuesday: 10-yard starts @ 90+% (3 sets, 60-second rest between sprints), 30-yard sprints @ 90% (3 sets, 60s rest between sprints).

Wednesday: power snatch (DE), front squat, (ME), good mornings (RE), standing military press (RE), seated cable rows (RE), hanging leg raises (RE).

Thursday: 60-yard sprints @ 80–85% (3 sets, 90s rest between sprints), 100-yard sprints @ 80–85% (3 sets, 90s rest between sprints).

Friday: push-press (DE), back squat (ME), glute-ham raises (RE), seated dumbbell presses (RE), chin-ups (RE), Russian twists (RE).
Saturday: 400-yard sprints @ 80% (3 sets, 5-minute rest between sets).
Sunday: Off.

[ME = Maximal Effort   DE = Dynamic Effort   RE = Repetition Effort]

This is a sample 4-week training block. On the speed training days, I usually increase the volume by one set each week, returning to three sets on week four. The percentage is relative to a scale of perceived exertion. For example, a sprint at 85 percent should feel like you are running at top speed, just short of an all out effort. Intensity and volume for weight lifting is also progressively waved up and down, depending on the progressive and physical readiness of each athlete.

OFF-SEASON TIPS*

In the off-season, focus on improving your body's ability to move, namely your strength, speed, quickness, and flexibility. Stronger muscles that are still flexible combined with improved movement techniques (both straight ahead and while changing direction) will make you a better athlete.

EVALUATE YOUR PAST SEASON

Ask yourself how well you played, where you were the strongest and where you need to improve. Your coach and teammates can be a big help. Make a list of the areas that need improvement. Next, write down how you plan to improve on those areas. If you found yourself being outrun, you may need to complete more sprints or work on your technique. If you need to hold your ground more effectively, spend time getting stronger in the weight room. Once you have made your list, prioritize your workouts to allow for time to work on those specific areas.

GET BUSY

Try to complete workouts on four or five days each week. These workouts should include two to three total body lifts along with some general conditioning as well as specific drills to improve your speed and quickness on at least three or four days each week. Remember, work from your core out. Your core is essentially the center of your body and is involved in every movement you perform on the field. It includes all the muscles between your ribs and your hips. You can emphasize your

---

*By Chris Endlich (Johns Hopkins strength and conditioning coach)

core by either performing exercises that directly work those muscles, such as sit-ups, bicycles, and back extensions, or indirectly, such as single-arm or single-leg exercises.

Since lacrosse is played while on your feet the bulk of your exercises for all muscle groups should be performed while standing up. Include exercises while standing on one leg or that just use one arm at a time. It doesn't hurt to include some of the more traditional exercises, such as a bench press or squat, but make them more difficult by doing your bench press on a physioball or complete the same squat on one leg, for example.

Lacrosse is a fast-moving sport full of constant change of direction. You rarely jog on the field so don't spend much time jogging during your off-season. If you practice running slow, you will get better at running slow; and you want to get faster, not slower! If you want to get faster running full field, then practice running full-field sprints, but spend most of your time working on your ability to change direction. A simple way to do this is to pick any letter of the alphabet and set up enough cones to form the letter on a field; you don't actually have to form the letter with a ton of cones, you just need enough to make the points of the letter. For example, the letter "M" would require five cones, one at each point. Once you have made your letter, start at one end of the letter and go through various movements to trace out the letter as if you are writing the letter with your running pattern; include sprints, backpedals, and slides in various orders. For example, the letter M has four movements: you can sprint through all four, slide through all four, or combine two or three of the movements, such as a sprint to a backpedal or a slide to a sprint. Pick two or three different letters each time, and spend about 10 minutes going through each. The distance between the cones can vary anywhere from as little as 2 or 3 yards to as much as 10 or 15 yards.

Although lifting and conditioning workouts are crucial, don't forget other often neglected areas such as flexibility. Be sure to thoroughly warm up using various movement stretches and form running. After your workout, finish with slower stretches where you hold each stretch for 10 seconds or so.

The next neglected area? Quick reaction ability. Improve this through various hand-eye coordination exercises, such as juggling, or using reaction balls (available on the Internet). Another effective drill: a card toss. Using a deck of ordinary playing cards, have a partner toss a card up while you try to catch it. Alternate using your right and left hand for as many cards as you want to do at a time, then switch positions and have your partner catch the cards that you throw.

Finally, leave time for recovery. You can lift all the weight and run all the sprints you want, but you must pay attention to your body. Give yourself enough time to rest, and make sure you are eating enough quality food and drinking enough water to properly fuel your muscles. Injuries, fatigue, and illness are oftentimes the result of not eating properly, as well as not getting enough rest. Take care of your body, and it will take care of you!

BIBLIOGRAPHY

American Indian Lacrosse (Thomas Vennum, Jr., The Smithsonian Institution, 1994)

Baffled Parent's Guide to Coaching Boys' Lacrosse (Greg Murrel and Jim Garland, McGraw-Hill, 2002)

Baffled Parent's Guide to Girls' Lacrosse (Janine Tucker, McGraw-Hill, 2003)

Boys' Lacrosse 2006 Rules Book (National Federation of State High School Associations)

Clear from the Crease (Bob Merrick, Lacrosse Foundation, 1982)

Coaching Youth Lacrosse, 2nd Edition (American Sport Education Program, Human Kinetics Publishers, 2003)

The Composite Guide to Lacrosse (Lois Nicholson, Chelsea House Publishers, 1999)

The Double-Goal Coach: Positive Coaching Tools for Honoring the Game and Developing Winners in Sports and Life (Jim Thompson, HarperCollins, 2003)

Lacrosse: A History of the Game (Donald M. Fisher, Johns Hopkins University Press, 2002)

Lacrosse for Dummies (Jim Hinkson, John Jiloty, and Robert Carpenter, John Wiley & Sons, 2003)

Lacrosse: Fundamentals for Winning (Bob Woodward and David Urick, Sports Illustrated Books, 1988)

Lacrosse Goaltending for Coaches (and Players) (Jon Weston, Weston Lacrosse, 1997)

NCAA Men's Lacrosse Rules (Charles W. Winters, NCAA, 2003)

Positive Coaching (Jim Thompson, Warde Publishers, 1995)

Sports Nutrition Guidebook (Nancy Clark, Human Kinetics Publishers, 2003)

The Strength and Conditioning Journal (periodical)

Stretching: 20th Anniversary Revised Edition (Bob Anderson, Shelter Publications, 2000)

Supertraining, 6th Edition (Mel Siff, Supertraining Institute, 2003)

US Lacrosse Publications

Lacrosse Magazine (eight issues/year)

Parents Guide to the Sport of Lacrosse, 11th Edition (2005)

Women's Rules 2005: Official Rules for Girls & Women's Lacrosse (2006)

Resources

US Lacrosse, Inc.
US Lacrosse Foundation
113 West University Parkway
Baltimore, MD 21210
(410) 235-6882
uslacrosse.org
laxmagazine.com
Also see: Uslia.com (United
States Lacrosse Intercollegiate
Associates)

Canadian Lacrosse Association
2211 Riverside Dr.
Suite B-4
Ottawa, ON K1H 7X5
(613)-260-2028
Lacrosse.ca

Human Kinetics
P.O. Box 5076
Champaign, IL 61825-5076
(800)-747-4457
humankinetics.com

Inside Lacrosse Magazine
(11issues/year)
701 East Pratt St. Suite 100
Baltimore,MD 21202
(410)-583-8180
insidelacrosse.com

**International Lacrosse
Federation (Men's)**
92 Chapel Rd., Moorabbin,
Victoria, Australia 3189
(613) 9555-7753
Intlaxfed.org

**International Federation of
Women's Lacrosse Association**
Fiona Clarke (President)
51 B Southern Cross Circle
Ocean Reef
Western Australia 6027
H: 08 9 300 4038
M: 0409 290 503
Womenslacrosse.org

Major League Lacrosse (MLL)
Brighton Landing East
20 Guest St., Suite 125
Boston, MA 02135
(617) 746-9980
Majorleaguelacrosse.com

**National Association
of Sport Officials (NASO)**
2017 Lathrop Ave.
Racine, WI 53405
(262) 632-5448
Naso.org

**NCAA (National Collegiate
Athletic Association)**
700 W. Washington St.
P.O. 6222
Indianapolis, IN 46206-6222
(317) 917-6222
ncaa.org
ncaasports.com

National Federation of State High School Associations (NFHS)
P.O. Box 690
Indianapolis, IN 46206
(317) 972-6900
nfhs.org

National Lacrosse League (NLL)
9 East 45th St., 5th floor
NY, NY 10017
(212) 764-1390
(917) 510-9200
nll.com

Positive Coaching Alliance Department of Athletics
Stanford University
Stanford, CA 94305-6150
(650) 725-0024
positivecoach.org

Pro Strength
Coach, Brian Yeager
2239 Napfle Street
Philadelphia, PA 19152
(267) 973-7493
prostrength.net

ADDITIONAL WEB SITES

E-lacrosse.com
Laxauction.com
Laxcamps.com
Laxdrills.com

TRAINING DVDs

The Third Team on the Field
(US Lacrosse MDOC Introductory Training Video)

Winning Lacrosse: Skills & Drills for the Beginning Player (with Jeff Tambroni, Head Coach, Cornell University)
(Chalk Talk Productions, 2005)

EQUIPMENT AND CLOTHING MANUFACTURERS

Ballgirl Athletic
225 West Chester Avenue
Port Chester NY 10573.
(877) 268-7778
ballgirlathletic.com

Brine, Inc.
47 Summer St.
Milford, Massachusetts 01757
(800) 227-2722
(508) 478-3250
Brinelax.com

Cascade Lacrosse
4635 Crossroads Park Dr.
Liverpool, NY 13088
(800) 537-1702
Cascadelacrosse.com

Custom-lax
(877) 884-8568
Custom-lax.com

Harrow
600 West Bayaud Ave.
Denver, Colorado 80223
(800) 541-2905
Harrowsports.com

Interlax
185 Pine Haven Shore Rd.
Shelburne, VT 05482
(802) 353-9155
Inter-lax.com

Maverick Lacrosse
1565 Franklin Ave., Suite 110
Mineola NY 11501
(516) 281-3048
Mavericklacarosse.com

Mohawk International Lacrosse
USA:
Box 13
Rooselvetown, NY 13683
(613) 936-1175
Canada:
RR#3
Cornwall Island, Ontario
Via Mohawk Nation
K6H 5R7
Mohawkintlacrosse.com

Proboss Lacrosse
1080 Brock Rd.
Pickering, Ontario
Canada L1W 3H3
(877) 4PB-LAXX
(905) 837-8326
Probosslacrosse.com

RefShop
(877) REF-S111
Refshop.com

Riddell Lacrosse
17 Farinella Dr.
East Hanover, NJ 07936
(973) 884-4880
(800) 308-4529
Riddelllacrosse.com

Rock-it Pocket
5609 Big Horn Crossing
Fort Collins, CO 80526
(970) 377-1390
(800) 374-7468
rock-itpocket.com

Shamrock Lacrosse
17 Fairnella Drive
East Hanover NJ. 07936
(973) 884-4880
Shamrocklax.com

Shock Doctor
3405 Annapolis Lane North
Plymouth, MN 55447
(800) 233-6956
Shockdoc.com

STX Lacrosse
1500 Bush Street
Baltimore, Maryland 21230
(800) 368-2250
(410) 837-2022
stxlacrosse.com

Tru Mark Athletic Field Marker
P.O. Box 706
Norfolk, NE 68702-0706
(800) 553-MARK (6275)
AthleticFieldMarker.com

Under Armour Performance Apparel
1010 Swan Creek Drive
Baltimore, MD 21226
(888) 7ARMOUR
Underarmour.com

Warrior Lacrosse
6881 Chicago Road
Warren, MI 48092
(586) 978-2595
(800) 968-7845
Warriorlacrosse.com

INDEX

METRIC EQUIVALENTS
[to the nearest mm, 0.1cm, or 0.01m]

INCHES	MM	CM	INCHES	MM	CM	INCHES	MM	CM
⅛	3	0.3	9	229	22.9	30	762	76.2
¼	6	0.6	10	254	25.4	31	787	78.7
⅜	10	1.0	11	279	27.9	32	813	81.3
½	13	1.3	12	305	30.5	33	838	83.8
⅝	16	1.6	13	330	33.0	34	864	86.4
¾	19	1.9	14	356	35.6	35	889	88.9
⅞	22	2.2	15	381	38.1	36	914	91.4
1	25	2.5	16	406	40.6	37	940	94.0
1 ¼	32	3.2	17	432	43.2	38	965	96.5
1 ½	38	3.8	18	457	45.7	39	991	99.1
1 ¾	44	4.4	19	483	48.3	40	1016	101.6
2	51	5.1	20	508	50.8	41	1041	104.1
2 ½	64	6.4	21	533	53.3	42	1067	106.7
3	76	7.6	22	559	55.9	43	1092	109.2
3 ½	89	8.9	23	584	58.4	44	1118	111.8
4	102	10.2	24	610	61.0	45	1143	114.3
4 ½	114	11.4	25	635	63.5	46	1168	116.8
5	127	12.7	26	660	66.0	47	1194	119.4
6	152	15.2	27	686	68.6	48	1219	121.9
7	178	17.8	28	711	71.1	49	1245	124.5
8	203	20.3	29	737	73.7	50	1270	127.0

CONVERSION FACTORS

1 mm	=	0.039 inch
1 m	=	3.28 feet
1 m²	=	10.8 square feet
1 inch	=	25.4 mm
1 foot	=	304.8 mm
1 square foot	=	0.09 m²
mm	=	millimeter
cm	=	centimeter
m	=	meter
m²	=	square meter